DANCE NAKED

DANCE
NAKED

A GUIDE TO UNLEASHING
YOUR INNER HOTTIE

Jessica "Kayla" Conrad

HARMONY BOOKS
NEW YORK

Published by Harmony Books, New York, New York.
Member of the Crown Publishing Group, a division of Random House, Inc.
www.crownpublishing.com

HARMONY BOOKS is a registered trademark and the Harmony Books colophon is a trademark of Random House, Inc.

Printed in the United States of America

Design by Karen Minster

Library of Congress Cataloging-in-Publication Data
Conrad, Jessica.
  Dance naked : a guide to unleashing your inner hottie /
  by Jessica "Kayla" Conrad.—1st ed.
  1. Striptease—Vocational guidance. 2. Striptease. I. Title.
  PN1949.S7C66 2004
  792.7—dc22

                                                    2003025026

ISBN 1-4000-5273-4

10 9 8 7 6 5 4 3 2 1

First Edition

This book is dedicated
to all girls who
just want to have fun

ACKNOWLEDGMENTS

First I'd like to thank my husband for his quiet, if somewhat befuddled, support. I'd also like to thank my son, for being the cutest, sweetest, smartest little boy in the world.

I'd also like to thank my agent, Paul S. Levine; my editor, Kim Kanner Meisner; and Shaye Areheart, for their support and encouragement.

Finally, I'd like to give an extra special, big, huge thank-you to Rachel Francis, who was with me in the trenches, and without whose friendship, feedback, and use of apartment I could never have written this book; and to Dr. Bernard Gertler, who, as testament to his talent, I have come to believe is a friend.

Contents

DANCE NAKED

Introduction

You slink toward the stage, hips first. They're all waiting for you. You can feel it. You can feel how much they want you, every inch of you—your hair, your eyes, your skin—just to see you, to look at you for a minute until you disappear, like an apparition into the smoke. It's almost too much; it's almost unfair. You almost feel sorry for them—they're only men, after all. You take a breath and push the door open. Suddenly, you are blinded by the glare of the stage lights, brighter than a million flashbulbs going off. The audience holds its breath. *The star has arrived.* The music pulses in your ears, in your blood. You feel every beat caress you, as your body begins to move, slowly, rhythmically, in time with the music.

And then you become aware that he's there. You know . . . *him.* The one who thought . . . thought he knew you. But he didn't. He didn't and doesn't know who you are, what's inside you, or what you're capable of. How you can burn the club down just by wishing it. And as you slowly peel down the top of your dress, you can sense him standing there, shocked, awed, humbled by your beauty and your power. He watches, and you pause, nearly frozen as he approaches the stage. He holds up a hundred-dollar bill, and as you lean over to accept his tip you hear him whisper, "Remember to get my All-Bran. You know what happens to me if I don't eat it every morning . . ." Your husband's quizzical frown comes into view as you stand in your kitchen, absently spreading peanut butter on a slice of wheat.

The stripper fantasy *is* a rather potent one. I know this first-hand as a dancer and as a witness: At least once a night, at the club where I work, a nondancer from the audience jumps up onstage and takes her clothes off. So what is it about the stripper fantasy that would cause an otherwise mild-mannered accounts manager to knock over the hapless girl onstage and peel off her Ann Taylor suit as if it were a Kathie Lee Collectible instead?

On a very real level, dancing is a job, just like any other, with the same perks and stressors. Except that we're almost naked, of course. The difference is that most women don't have default fantasies about being account executives or writing R&D reports. But every woman, at least once, wants to know what it feels like to make her man dissolve into a puddle of tears, apologies, and longing. She wants to know what it feels like to take her clothes off for an adoring audience or maybe just for Ben Affleck. To make her man sit up and beg like the hound dog he is. And when you think about it, who doesn't want to be the girl who gets the five-hundred-dollar tip from George Clooney or Ethan Hawke? It's fun!

Every woman has an inner hottie that is dying to be unleashed. Even the most politically conservative, Wal-Mart-shopping, coupon-clipping soccer mom (you know who you are) is wearing a French-lace demicup bustier with matching garter underneath her pima cotton smock. A trip to the strip club offers a woman a safe environment to throw off the smock and reveal her hidden goddess.

Since strip clubs are all about fantasy, it's important that we first clear up a few misconceptions about strippers and strip clubs to help distinguish fact from fiction.

THE TOP SIX MISCONCEPTIONS ABOUT STRIPPERS

I.   We're Nymphos

I guess it's an easy assumption to make, given that our job is to gyrate in front of men wearing just a G-string and a smile. It's not too much of a stretch to imagine that sexy girls dancing in sexy clothes would lead to sexy thoughts and acts. The truth, however, is that dancing is boring. Yes, boring. Doing the same dance, song after song, night after night, for the same sort of men gets . . . boring. Strippers work really hard to mask this, especially when giving a dance, because the last thing we want is for our customers to realize that they put us to sleep. We'll laugh, joke, chat it up, or just fantasize that we're really dancing for Brad Pitt, to keep an interested look on our faces and stay awake.

2.   We're Hookers

You, as a civilian (nonstripper), might not be clear on where the line between stripping and hooking is, but believe me, we are. Dancers aren't hookers. Dancers aren't women who strip and occasionally hook. Dancers do not get paid to have any form of sexual contact with a customer. Dancers do not have any kind of sex with customers, or any kind of sex with each other in front of customers. No hand jobs, no blow jobs, no phone jobs. No grinding into a customer's lap with such friction and force that he "finishes," or whatever. Which brings us to a related misconception:

3. We're Desperate

Dancers are not forlorn wayfarers cast about by the sea of life. We do not become dancers because we want love, acceptance, or self-esteem. We become dancers because we want money. Dancing makes good business sense. Depending on the club and the city it's in, a dancer can easily clear one hundred thousand dollars a year. That's a lot more than the starting salary of most women with MBAs. So, you see, this is why we are not hookers: We don't need to be. In the VIP room, dancers get paid upwards of four hundred dollars an hour to sit, sip champagne, and dance in a safe, protected environment with *absolutely no physical contact* with the customer. That's more than most lawyers, doctors, or shrinks make, for a lot less work.

4. We Come from Broken Homes

Or crack houses. Or broken crack houses. The truth is that sure, every strip club has its own version of Whitney Houston or Courtney Love. You know, the really skinny, scary chick who staggers around looking like she needs to be put on medication. But, then again, so does *every* job. If you look around, chances are there's someone who's a little too fond of the song "White Lines" sitting in the office next to yours.

5. We're Degraded

A popular critique of dancing is that it's degrading to women. All right. I'll buy it. But then tell me this: What job isn't degrading to women? Before I became a dancer, I spent five years in investment banking. Personally, I found it far more degrading to be asked to fax, photocopy, or type something for a guy getting paid five times my salary who was too busy looking up porn on the Internet to get off his lazy ass and do it himself. It was even more degrading to find my boss's expense report and see that he was more than happy to spend two thousand dollars in *one night* at a strip club but wouldn't give me a two-thousand-dollar-*a-year* raise. That, my friends, is degrading.

6. We're Stupid

The final piece of stripper fiction is that we're so dumb only a strip club *would* hire us. Well, as you have seen, dancing does make good business sense, so it shouldn't come as a surprise that a lot of dancers have a bachelor's degree, several more even have some kind of advanced degree. Further, a good percentage of those who don't are currently putting their dancing dollars toward tuition. Others choose to invest their hard-earned money in the stock market, real estate, restaurants, clubs, and other businesses. So there are a lot of really smart reasons to dance—reasons that only a smart woman would know.

~~~~~

Well, there you have it—people's biggest misconceptions about strippers. To be fair, I'm sure some dancers *are* nymphomaniac hookers who are desperate, come from broken crack homes, and are degraded at the job because they are just too painfully stupid to care. Then again, I'm sure you've all had at least one boss or coworker who also fit that description.

Now that we've covered the fiction of stripping, let's move on to the facts.

OH, BEHAVE! THE 411 ON MEN

Sharing the planet with men has its upside and its downside. On the upside, we'll always have someone on taking-out-the-garbage and bug-squashing duty. We also get someone who is preternaturally attuned to cars and has strong hands for back rubs. On the downside, we actually have to hear what men say. Which is why it's easy to imagine, having been subjected to a lifetime of wolf whistles and catcalls on the street, that men are even more annoying in the strip club. Most people think that men at strip clubs behave like the damn dirty apes they are. Not true!

Here are the surprising facts about men:

1.   They're Polite

Strip clubs are a little like amusement parks: There are lots of attractions, rides, and games, but they can also be kind of overwhelming. And a dancer, instead of being like the helpful guide dressed up in a Goofy costume waiting to point you in the right direction, is really more like the pickpocket waiting to take advantage of your befuddlement. In any other situation where someone tries to turn you upside down to shake the last piece of lint out of your pocket, you get irritated. But because men get to see lots of naked boobs while they're being shaken down, they're usually polite, well mannered, and kind.

2. They're Respectful

Most strip clubs have strict no-touching policies and large beefy bouncers to enforce them. However, even when the customer (or stripper) is drunk and no one's watching, men *still* don't touch. So give a hand to moms everywhere—they're still teaching their boys to behave. Unfortunately, the same cannot be said for our female customers. Which brings us to:

OH, BEHAVE! THE 411 ON WOMEN

1. Chicks Dig Getting Dances Too

Women come to strip clubs alone, in groups, with male and female coworkers, and as part of a couple. Not because they were dragged in by their husbands or boyfriends, but because they love getting dances. One of my best friend's customers was a beautiful lesbian who would come into the club once a month and spend hundreds of dollars getting dances. I also had a terrific customer who was a woman (a married gynecologist!) who would come in every so often to have me dance for her.

2. Women Are Animals

I'm not sure if it's because women are socialized to repress themselves, or if it's because they're drunk—either way, when women get a lap dance, they will grope, paw, and generally try to get away with as much as they possibly can without being tossed out by a bouncer. They're uncaged beasts!

Who would think, going into a strip club, that dancers are smart, men are polite, and women are all hands?

Lastly, it's important to note here, in the Introduction, that I am in no way claiming that dancing is the greatest job in the world. Nor am I advocating that all women quit their day jobs at once to begin their new, exciting careers as professional lap dancers. Unless, of course, they want to. It worked for me, but I'm the exception, not the rule. Dancing, like any other job, has its good and bad points. Good points: money, freedom, self-confidence. Bad points: being asked nightly whether I *like* (i.e., have sex with) the women I work with, whether I shave or wax, and, of course, what my phone number is. While I can't deny that some aspects of stripping trouble me, I also can't deny that I have benefited tremendously from having danced—certainly financially, but more importantly, personally. My self-confidence has increased, and I have come to own and appreciate my sexuality in ways that would not have happened had I not been a dancer. In this vein, this book will teach you the valuable lessons I have learned from my expertise as a dancer, without the messy actually-having-to-be-a-stripper part.

Each chapter is devised to be one of the six steps you'd take on your journey to becoming a stripper. In the first chapter, "Live

(Nearly) Nude Girls," we will explore why people think dancers are so sexy and what it actually is that makes them so. In chapter 2, "Bootylicious!" we'll talk about the insecurities and doubts all women (including dancers) have and what tools dancers use to overcome them. In chapter 3, "Glama Slama," you will learn the top-secret hair and makeup tricks dancers use to get that patented supersexy look. We'll discuss what products to use, where to get them, and how to apply them. Chapter 4, "Stripper Chic," will show you what to wear when you want to inject a little stripper spice into your wardrobe. We'll also pick out what clothes you'll want to take off for your man. Chapter 5, "The Big Tease," is all about attitude. You will learn the formal techniques dancers use to pry dollars out of men's tight little paws to win valuable cash and prizes of your own! Finally, after mastering steps 1 through 5, in chapter 6, "Alias: Hottie," you will choose a stripper name of your own, to unleash at will. It is time, Grasshopper. You have earned it.

Included within each chapter are exercises to do at home. Like any other self-improvement program, no pain, no gain. If you really want to explore that dark alley where your inner hottie has been hiding out, wearing black eyeliner and a leather mini, biding her time smoking cloves and mugging men for kisses, you need to subscribe to the "exercise" program. These exercises will take you through the basics of learning how to feel comfortable in your own naked skin and then, once you do, relearning how to dress it.

A FINAL NOTE: Have fun!

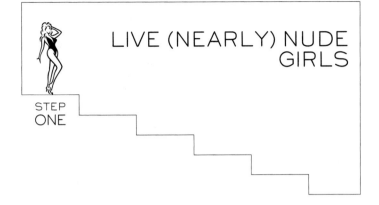

LIVE (NEARLY) NUDE GIRLS

STEP ONE

Most people think that strippers are hot because they have perfect, surgically created cookie-cutter bodies. The fact is that dancers, like "real" women, come in all shapes and sizes: top-heavy, bottom-heavy, top- *and* bottom-heavy, muscular, toned, and even doughy. Some strippers' faces are beautiful, some cute, and some have the same random noses or recessive chins that other women have. Most are tan, some are pale. Some have long hair, some short. All but the smallest minority have cellulite and stretch marks somewhere on their bodies. If strippers are so much like ordinary women, then, why does everyone think they're so hot?

The truth is, what really makes a stripper hot is simply her willingness to get naked for you. It's that spark, that moment of utter abandon when a stripper begins her dance, that makes her absolutely, smoking hot. Contained within that spark, that instant, is a sense of complete self-confidence and self-possession. A total owning of her sexuality and power that says, Sit back, Sparky, Mama's taking you for a ride.

So why is it that some women, like strippers, are totally okay letting complete strangers see them nearly naked, while the rest of us cringe at the thought? Where does a stripper's self-confidence come from?

This one's easy: A dancer's self-confidence comes from having a deep level of comfort with her body that ordinary women don't have. The real question is, why *don't* ordinary women have the same deep level of comfort with their bodies that dancers do?

To really understand how some stripping experience boosts your self-confidence, you really have to understand that strippers are strictly a product of their environment. Dancers are made, not born. No woman has ever decided to dance because she was so painfully hot that she felt duty-bound to show it to any man willing to pay a small fee. No woman has ever become a dancer because she was just too sexy or smokin' to do anything else. Dancers are comfortable being seen naked because for us it's the norm. We're a product of our culture, just like you.

CULTURE CLUB

In a way it's a good thing that most of us don't like to be seen naked, because in the United States, public nudity is not only frowned upon, it's (usually) downright illegal. You can get fined or even arrested for nude sunbathing *in your own backyard*. If the law is this hard on your behavior on your own private property, you can well imagine how much more strict it is if you attempt to get naked anywhere else—the sidewalk or the grocery store, for instance. Actually, a few years ago a group of women sued New York State after being arrested for walking around topless at a festival in Rochester. The women, who called themselves the Topfree Seven, argued that men walk around topless all the time without getting thrown in jail, and that women ought to be given the same rights. The court agreed, and now, just so you know, in case you want to, it is perfectly legal for a woman to sunbathe in Central Park, eat at an outdoor café, and stroll the city streets wearing nothing on top but a whole lot of sunscreen. As of this writing, no one has taken New York City up on its timely recognition of gender equality by actually doing any of this. Why? Well, it's just weird. Can you imagine being the only woman in a city of eight million people walking around with your boobs just out there for anyone to see? You window-shopping, while others politely pretend not to look at you? It's kind of horrible—a lot like those omigod-I'm-giving-a-presentation-and-I-don't-have-any-pants-on dreams that plague all of us from time to time.

Now imagine that, for some reason, walking around topless in New York City became all the rage, and that instead of spending thousands of dollars on knockoffs of what Carrie from *Sex and the City* wore last season, all the annoying fashionistas decided that nothing was quite as chic as nothing at all. Big boobs, little boobs, perky boobs, saggy boobs, pretty boobs, ugly boobs, all just swinging around. At first it'd be a complete shock. Then, after a while, it'd become the norm. Just like you'd expect to see topless women on the beaches of Saint-Tropez and South America, you'd come to expect to see topless women on the subway in New York City. No one would think twice about it.

As strange as it sounds, this is what a strip club is like. It's an alternate universe. Not quite Bizarro World, but something like it. And actually this bizarre parallel universe does exist. It's called . . . Europe.

Nothing drives home the acute differences between American women's and European women's attitudes toward nudity more than working at a strip club. Most clubs have women from all over the world who work as dancers—Armenian, Brazilian, Bulgarian, Czech, Dutch, English, Finnish, Georgian, Israeli, Italian, Polish, Portuguese, Puerto Rican, and Russian, to name just a few. Of course, every woman comes to dancing for her own individual reasons, but it's interesting to note that most European women have no complex nudity issues or internal debates about right/wrong, good/bad, or sinner/saint. Regardless of their religious beliefs or upbringing, European women tend to have fewer issues with public nudity or, more importantly, their own. They just come in, work hard, and go home. The point I'm making here is that our attitudes about nudity are largely influenced by our culture, and that a strip club has its own unique culture that enables even the most prudish women to open up and feel comfortable nekkid.

When you break it down, there are five important ways the strip club makes the stripper:

I.   All Nude, All the Time

Okay. I need to make a clarification right here. While it's true that some strip clubs do feature all-nude dancers, the club where I work does not. I do not and have not ever danced completely nude. Oh, well, except when I've just gotten out of the shower and my husband and two-year-old aren't around. And in that case, yes, I do dance completely nude sometimes. Anyway, in this chapter and throughout this book, when I say *nude* or *naked*, I'm really talking about being *nearly* naked—that is, wearing a G-string, high heels, and a garter. Alrighty, then. Moving on.

The first and most important reason why dancers are comfortable with their bodies is that they spend forty hours a week naked. Whether it's onstage, dancing for a customer, getting ready in the dressing room, eating dinner, or just having a chat, we're pretty much all naked, all the time. Okay, we're not really naked, as I've just explained, but we're as close to it as you can possibly get without losing our liquor license. To find out exactly why spending so much naked time increases a stripper's sexiness, let's first take the sex out of it.

As I mentioned in the Introduction, one of the misconceptions about dancers is that we're nymphos, and that we only dance for a living because we're too horny all the time to work at oh, say . . . McDonald's. I then went on to say that dancing could actually be quite boring. Which is absolutely true. For strippers, giving a dance isn't about being sexual. It's about work. Shaking our hooters and smacking our asses is just part of the job description. Giving a dance is about as sexual as typing up a progress report, and every bit as monotonous, too. You see, each dancer has a choreographed dance she does every single song, for every single customer, every single time. If we are asked to give a second dance, we just do it all again, backward. (FYI: It's the basic striptease, the steps to which you'll learn for yourself at the end of this chapter.) The dance doesn't flow out of our irrational sexual exuberance—it's carefully calculated so that you get to see what you came in for before the dance is over. So just ignore what the look on a dancer's face is telling you, or what she's whispering in your ear. There are only three things strippers think about while we're giving a dance: 1) Can I get this guy into the VIP room? 2) How much money have I made so far? and 3) Have I shown him my butt yet? So, you see, even though dancers spend a lot of time naked, it's in the *nonsexual* context of being at work.

This just so happens to be the exact opposite of what civilian women do. In fact, most women only get naked *for* sex or, at least, sex-related activities. Think about it: If the only time you spend naked is in the shower shaving your legs and pits in case your man comes over, or getting dressed to look good for getting undressed for sex, then that means the only time you spend naked is time you are worrying about looking good for or pleasing your man. For most women, then, being naked comes unnecessarily weighted with a lot of anxiety and pressure. This influences even our forays into clothes shopping. If we're not trying to look good for our man, we're often trying to look good because of the judgments of other women. Either way, when you're worried about looking good for someone else, it's impossible to feel good about yourself. For dancers, once we're out on the floor working, we don't have time to obsess over whether we look okay. We just do the best we can, trust that it's good enough, let go, and get to work. By being naked so often, we become familiar with our bodies in a nonjudgmental way. This familiarity leads to a feeling of comfortableness. We feel confident taking our clothes off because we are comfortable with our naked bodies—we have nothing to hide. For you, then, the more you can remove the time you spend naked from a sexual context, or any context where you are worried about the judgments of others, the more you will feel comfortable with your body as it is. Ideally, seeing yourself au naturel should become second nature. You should be intimately familiar with your naked body, how it looks, and how it functions in all sorts of conditions and situations, not just sexual ones. Ask yourself: What do my naked thighs look like in the kitchen or in the basement? What does my belly do when I'm not sucking it in or covering it up? When we really get to know and respect our bodies is when we will stop dragging them around like the freaky friend we're too embarrassed to be seen with in public in case she does something weird. You should be so used to yourself that you become as unaware of your naked-ness as a stripper is. The following exercises will help you to do it.

EXERCISE: MAKING NAKED TIME

1. Pick a chore you do around the house, when you are alone. Maybe it's washing the breakfast dishes after you pack the kids off to school. Maybe it's putting in a load of laundry, clipping coupons, or filing old bills. Find a chore you feel comfortable with, then take off your clothes and do it naked. It may seem ridiculous, but as I've said, strippers do boring, mundane things like eating dinner naked every day. You only need to do this exercise once to realize how different the dancer's attitude toward nudity and the average woman's is. If you're like most, the mere *idea* of going down to the basement naked to put in a load of laundry should be scandalous.

2. Everyone has time to sleep naked. If this is not something you ordinarily do, your man might take it as an invitation for sex, in which case you should have it, if you'd like. If it seems too abrupt a change from your ordinary full-length flannel nighties, begin slowly. For example, start with a T-shirt and jammy pants, then move on to a tank top and shorts. Gradually remove your clothing, week by week and piece by piece, until you feel comfortable falling asleep and spending a full night nude. Extra points if you include bedtime rituals you might have, such as reading a book or writing in a journal. The more naked time you spend, the more comfortable with your body you will feel.

After you've done at least one of these exercises, examine your thoughts and feelings about them. Did you feel uncomfortable or silly? Did you feel free? Or naughty? If you can, try exercise 1 a few times, until it becomes normal to do whichever chore you chose naked. This will jump-start your comfortableness with your own skin in a way that agonizing and analyzing never will.

2.   Dance Naked

Now we're ready to add the sex back into it. Dancing is sexy. Dancing with unbridled abandon to a song you love is one of the most fun, freeing, joyful, and erotic experiences in the world. Even those people who claim they hate dancing secretly really love it. They're just scared to look like a total spaz in front of other people. Get them alone, in the privacy of their living room or shower or car, and they'll unleash their superfreak in less time than it takes to double-check that no one is looking. Love for dancing crosses all cultural, ethnic, financial, and generational bounds. Even churchgoing, cardigan-wearing Perry Como sang a song about getting all sweaty to the rhythms of the night in the 1950s hit song "Papa Loves Mambo." Sample lyric: "Look at 'em sway with it / Getting' so gay with it / Shoutin' 'olé' with it, wow!"

Way back when, before Hollywood decided that everything up to but not including the actual "money shot" was acceptable audience viewing, a dance sequence was always used to express the characters' physical attraction to each other. Many black-and-white films, no matter how serious the subject, inserted some random dance scene where the leads ended up at the same cotillion together. Dance was how characters showed their desire for each other. (The meaning of the dance sequence is not to be confused with the meaning of the inevitable train-in-tunnel firework montages.)

There is power in the dance. So it's no wonder it scares some people—or large segments of people, like entire towns. The movie *Footloose* was based on a true story. In fact, there are still some towns—Pound, Virginia, for example—where public dancing is illegal. One fervent churchgoer was quoted in the August 21, 2001, issue of the *Kingsport Times-News,* saying, "I can never see a time when dancing can be approved of, especially with people who are not married . . . Dancing is one of those things that entices. It imitates sexual contact." To quote Perry Como, *Wow!* It seems that people are *still* afraid of what naughty beasts might get unleashed through the power of dance. Which brings us to the naughtiest form of dance of all: the striptease. Dancing in just a G-string, the smallest slip of fabric, with the music pumping and the lights pulsing is sexy. Whether I'm dancing onstage or for a customer night after night, there is something about watching my (nearly) nude body move. I see my skin, golden and shimmery under the furtive lighting; I see my muscles move, supple, graceful in time with the music. I see my breasts, small, round, and ripe, sway along as I dance. It's a profoundly sensual experience. Let me be really specific here: *Dancing* is sexy. Dancing for a customer (unless it's Antonio Banderas) is not. Strippers do not get turned on dancing for some fat, middle-aged, potbellied drunk guy with bad breath and a worse comb-over. We get "turned on" by moving our beautiful, naked, and powerful bodies in a certain way.

So how does this add up? How is dancing both sexy and not sexy at the same time? It's a little complicated, but in the end it will make sense if you follow me. Spending so much time a week naked takes the shock value out of it. It stops being naughty, bad, or uncomfortable . . . it just *is*. Strippers don't feel self-conscious about being naked, because for us, being naked is normal. Just like for you, after some practice, doing the dishes or laundry naked would become normal too. When you stop feeling self-conscious, all that's left is you, alone, naked. For strippers, it's at this time that we're able to really appreciate how beautiful our bodies are. Because we're not self-consciousness, we're not critical, and therefore we are able to value our bodies instead. It's at this moment when we start to value our bodies that we are able to welcome how sexy we really are. And this is how it should work for you, too. Feeling sexy is not something you should turn on and off. To truly own your sexuality, you should feel deeply sexy all the time—regardless of how you look, what you weigh, where you are, what you're doing, or any other factors that might come into play.

EXERCISE: SHAKE IT UP

Make sure you are alone. Trust me, you don't want the kiddies walking in on this one.

Wear comfortable clothes, put on a song you love, and hit the repeat button. It can be an anthem that's irresistible to sing along to, like "Respect" or "I Will Survive," or something slower that makes you feel all tingly because it reminds you of the first time you went to third base. One of my favorite songs to dance to is Melissa Etheridge's "Like the Way I Do." I start crawling around on my hands and knees like a cat in heat when I play it. Oddly, my second favorite is "The Lion Sleeps Tonight" by the Tokens. The key is that you pick something you can lose yourself in. Then just sing, dance, and strip to the imaginary person in the chair.

Yell. Do a few high kicks. Grab your naked love handles and shake them. Peel off your sweatshirt and swing it over your head. Make sure you feel silly. Laugh. Cry. Do it over and over. Do you notice how sexy and unstoppable you feel?

3.   Sister Act

Remember the 2003 season of *Survivor: The Amazon*, where it was the men's Tambaqui tribe against the women's Jaburu tribe? (The one where that swimsuit model Jenna won the million and then made *another* million by posing for *Playboy*?) Well, a strip club is exactly like that. It's the dancers' team against the men's, and the goal is to outwit, outlast, and outplay each other to go home with the prize.

On one side you have the Strippers, all working toward the same exact goal: to make as much money as possible. On the other side you have the Customers, who can score against the dancers by one of three different plays: A) spend as little money as possible; B) get a dancer to agree to a date with him; or C) cop a grope or a feel if neither A nor B is possible. Sure, there is also some competition between strippers, but it's the kind that serves to spur each other on, not vote each other off. Strippers know that they are all in it together, competing *against men*—to win their wallets. We are *not* competing against *each other* for the man—or his wallet. No, no, no!

To the civilian, strippers seem to represent all the things that men find desirable in a woman. Because of this, many women feel threatened by dancers. They believe that we're all G-string divas who wouldn't think twice about stabbing them in the back with one of our five-inch heels. I think most women are scarred from experience. We've all liked the boy who didn't like us back, and we've all been devastated when he started dating the popular girl we hated. We've all had that horrible feeling of seeing our boyfriend check out another woman, even though we've spent an hour getting dressed and look really good. Most of us have been cheated on by someone over the course of our romantic history, and a goodly portion of us have been the ones that a man has done the cheating with. So it seems natural to feel a certain amount of animosity toward strippers who get paid twenty dollars a dance to be the other woman. But the truth is that what really happens backstage is that the dressing room mimics a team locker room; the girls are friendly, supportive of one another, and do whatever we can to help each other score (i.e., make money). Dancers have got each other's backs—in every way. This is how:

There is an I *in* stripper.

At a regular office, almost nobody truly likes teamwork, because it's really just a load of bull. Seriously. Everyone has his or her own agenda, whether it's to kiss the boss's keister, rise up the corporate ladder, or score a simple raise. Despite the "There's no *I* in *team*" talks and no matter how many irritating "Success" posters they put up, everyone is very much in it for themselves. Dancing is surprisingly different. First of all, we have no invest-ment in seeing another dancer fail. We don't make any more money if another dancer makes any less. It's actually the opposite. At a club, guys start spending only if other guys are spending. It's this weird unspoken communication thing that guys have going where they can just sort of sense when it's the right time to open up their wallets. The entire club can be jam-packed with people, and not one single customer will ask for a dance. It can stay this way for a frustratingly long time, until *boom!* One customer buys a dance and suddenly the room explodes with half-naked women throwing their clothes off everywhere. This means that if another dancer is making a killing out on the floor, chances are you will too. And in most cases it's actually easier to get a dance if two dancers approach a guy at once. Even if the same guy has said no to both dancers individually, the second they team up for what we call "double trouble," he'll buy a dance. Not only is it easier to get a guy to spend forty dollars on two strippers than twenty dollars on one, it's also sometimes easier to get him to spend eight hundred dollars an hour on two strippers in the VIP room than just four hundred dollars on one. Some dancers work better together than others, and the two dancers that men like in a pair may not necessarily like each other. Make no mistake, though: They *will* work together, encourage each other, and support each other in their moneymaking attempts. They will *not* undermine each other or, worse still, slag each other to the customer in hopes of taking all the money for themselves, because it doesn't work. It just makes the customer not like you, and then spend less money altogether.

EXERCISE: TEAM SPIRIT

Okay, I know you probably don't have time to join the local softball team. But you should. There is lots and lots of evidence that playing team sports has a positive developmental effect on girls. There's no reason this shouldn't also be true for grown women. If you have old injuries and can't see yourself out on the soccer field, try something that requires only mental exertion, like a chess or Scrabble club. Even Michelle Pfeiffer reportedly belongs to a bowling league . . . it wasn't her stunt double knocking down pins in *Grease 2*.

4. The Benjamins

Remember a few years ago when then-supermodel Linda Evangelista declared that she wouldn't get out of bed for less than ten thousand dollars a day? This one comment alone proved to be more annoying than being subjected to years of L'Oréal's "Don't Hate Me Because I'm Beautiful" ad campaigns, and as expected, there was a backlash. So a bunch of models banded together to say, Well, no, just because we're pretty doesn't mean we're vapid, and then they set about to prove it by posing naked for an antifur poster. While some animal activists picket research facilities and others go to jail, these chicks stuck to what they did best—they *modeled* in protest! They showed everyone by their disapproving pouts that fur is *bad.* Then they all took turns doing serious interviews saying how modeling isn't all it's cracked up to be. As if getting paid thousands of dollars a day just to look good didn't feel every bit as good as people think it does.

Having modeled (okay, it was a Japanese beer commercial, but it counts) and danced, I'm here to tell you that it absolutely does. It feels every bit as great to get paid to be good-looking as you might think it would. It's a little surreal to count out the twenties and realize that you have just made eight hundred dollars for doing nothing but showing a bunch of random guys your boobs. What makes it even better is that it doesn't matter whether you're PMSing or having a bad-hair day—men will want to see you naked anyway!

Civilian women don't get this kind of reinforcement. When you feel fat and ugly, you just feel . . . fat and ugly. There isn't a guy with a hundred-dollar bill standing in your kitchen waiting for you to give him a dance. There is no photographer shouting, "Yes!

Work it, baby! You are so hot my camera's on fire!" while you writhe around on your throw rugs. But imagine if there were. It's really not that much of a stretch, is it? I mean, there are petite models, regular models, and plus-size models; there are hair models, face models, hand and feet models. I had a friend who was actually a calf model (he modeled that part of his leg—not his pet baby farm animal). He made an extra thousand a month going in whenever male fitness magazines needed a model for certain leg exercises. There are models of every type, and models of every age—baby, teen, women, and older women. Chances are you, or at least some part of you, fits into one of these categories. If it's not practical or possible to run out and get your portfolio put together to try your luck in the lucrative world of knee modeling, you can still feel like a superstar. Here's how:

EXERCISE: WORK THAT RUNWAY

For this exercise, you'll need to find some time when you can be alone, have access to your CD player, and wear your highest pair of heels. Three-inch-plus is best, but gardening clogs will work if they're all you've got.

First, put on a CD. Pulsing techno is best, but anything with a fast beat will do. Turn it up as loud as you or your neighbors can stand and slip on your heels. Now get into position. The "cat-walk," or "runway," at a fashion show is broken down like a clock: Start position is six o'clock, the end of the runway is twelve o'clock, your left side is nine o'clock, and your right side is three o'clock. You generally want to start at six, hit twelve, ten, and two, do a twirl or two, and then head back to six. Got it? Okay. Let's start by getting on the six and adjusting your posture.

High heels tend to force you to arch your back. Fight this by tucking your pelvis under as far as you can, so that your pelvis, lower back, and rib cage form a concave arc. Finally, open your shoulders and arch your upper back as much as you can. You are now ready to strut down the catwalk. Extend each leg in front of you straight from your hip as you take each step. Once you get the hang of it, you'll find that this position causes you to walk really fast. Stop when you reach the end of the room and pose by jutting your hips out to one side. Throw a surly, pouty look at your imaginary audience. Turn and face the ten o'clock position. Stick out your other hip, and continue to pout. Turn back to twelve o'clock, then throw a hostile glance over at two o'clock. Do a turn if you want, keeping the intimidating stare all the while. Return to the start position, change your outfit, and do it again.

The great thing about the model walk is that it's an instant perk-me-up. Try it the next time you're schlumping through the cat-food section of the grocery store, and you'll see what I mean.

As you can imagine, it's just really hard to feel fat or ugly when you've got the five hundred dollars men have shoved into your garter for being a hottie. It's also hard to wallow when you see women with less toned bodies doing dance after dance while women with "perfect" bodies struggle to get a dance. The logic, Aristotle, goes like this: If people are paying to see you undressed, then you look good. End of story. Gradations are irrelevant. Sure, Madison might look better and Montana might look "worse," but men are still willing to pry open their sweaty little fingers and give you twenty dollars to see what you look like without your clothes on. Any of you.

5.   Rubber, Glue

In real life, rejection can be painful at best and devastating at worst. Rejection feels bad, whether it's getting passed over for a promotion or declined by a school. Rejection feels even worse when it's more personal—getting turned down by a guy we want to hook up with or by our husbands or partners. Rejection hurts. Despite what the "experts" say about how it shouldn't be taken personally and, even worse, the "it's not you it's them" thing, it's often impossible to not feel that any kind of rejection is highly personal. After all, it's you personally putting yourself out there, and you who are personally getting passed over. Rejection is even more upsetting when it comes to love. Most of us become familiar with it early in life, when we have a crush on the school football or baseball champ, who does not now and never will know of our existence. We all remember how it feels to watch the boy we secretly love and admire stride past with someone who is definitely *not* us on his arm.

Sadly, it only gets worse after we grow up and enter the animal world of actual dating. Most of us have shared the common experience of having gone on a fantastic date with someone who has never called us back; some of us have even had fantastic sex with the person from this fantastic date who has never called us back. Some of us have had the five-date "relationship" with someone where everything was going well, until your man, inexplicably, without a word or a phone call, dropped off the face of the earth.

Then there are the truly painful kinds of rejection, which all of us have experienced at least once: being dumped—kicked to the curb by someone we once thought loved us. Or, even worse, discovering that the person we thought loved and cared about us also loved and cared about someone else—because he was cheating. These occurrences are emotionally devastating and rightfully so. Some people have been so badly burned by experiences that they avoid dating altogether. And some people who have never personally felt the burn live in such fear and dread of it that they avoid dating altogether.

In the average woman's life, though, the number of times she has been rejected by someone she cares about is small compared with the number of positive, accepting experiences she has had. This is actually what makes rejection feel so horrible. The less you have been rejected, the worse it usually feels.

This is where some strip-club experience comes in handy. Over the course of one hour, a stripper will be rejected more times than you will be rejected over the course of your entire life. Hundreds of times. Literally. And, I'm sad to say, men aren't always pleasant about it either. As I've mentioned, most of the time men are polite. When we go up to a customer to ask if they want a dance, we'll usually get a simple "No, thanks" or a "Come back later" if they're not interested. Sometimes, however, men are unwittingly insulting. Here's one lovely way I was rejected. I had just come back to work after having my son. I had spent the three months of my maternity leave working out feverishly and had lost most of my baby weight—forty pounds, with ten left to go. Still, because I had been hitting the gym hard, I looked good. I was firm, tight, and toned.

It was early evening, and the club was empty. I sat down to chat with a customer in the hope of maybe getting a couple of dances or, if I was lucky, roping him into the VIP room and having a relaxed, easy night. The customer and I chatted for about ten minutes and then I asked him if he wanted a dance. He said he wasn't ready yet, so I stayed and chatted with him some more. After another ten minutes, I asked again, and he again said no. It dawned on me then that he was actually never going to ask me to dance for him. I wasn't angry—sometimes you're just not someone's type. Since he was a nice guy anyway, I asked him what kind of girl he was looking for. He looked me up and down, thought carefully a moment, and said, "I don't know—brown hair, *petite* . . ." Now, mind you, not only am I a brunette, but I had been petite my entire life. At five foot four and 110 pounds, I was always just shy of the doctor's recommendation for a healthy weight. I'd always been in good shape—I was just skinny. Now that I weighed 120 pounds (smack-dab in the middle of the healthy section on the weight chart) I was suddenly a *big* girl. Like I needed to shop in the plus-size stripper department. Of course, the customer didn't mean to insult me—he was just answering my question. And the hundred-dollar bill he gave me to find the perfect girl for him helped cushion the blow.

Other times, the rejection isn't so kind. Some men are intentionally rude. One especially ugly man said to a friend of mine, "I can tell you're over twenty-five by the way your ass sits on the back of your legs." *Slam!* Another friend of mine was asked, "How did you get hired here? Aren't your tits too small for you to be stripping?" *Pow!* Then there are the half-wits, Casanovas, and self-appointed connoisseurs who delight in telling you, "You're not even on my list." Like we care. It's not that rejection doesn't bother us—it certainly does. We're human beings, after all. It's just that it's such a part of the normal course of our job, we're used to it.

I want to add a little side note here about rejection. As a civilian, you might feel upset to learn that men are sometimes rude to dancers. It might also seem that dancers must have low self-esteem or a poor self-image if we put ourselves in a position to take it. Not so. First of all, as mentioned, it's actually pretty rare that a customer will be out-and-out rude to us. Even so, it's no more than what a man goes through in his dating life. If you think about it, women turn down men all the time. And women can be pretty rude about it too. It's just that as women, we're so used to being approached, hit on, and whistled and hollered at that we don't even notice how many times a day we do the rejecting. So it makes sense that it's slightly shocking to think about the situation in reverse. Here's an exercise you can read through or try, to get a better understanding of what I mean:

EXERCISE: WORST-CASE SCENARIO

Sit down somewhere quiet and do the following: Imagine you are a dancer at a club. You are dressed to the nines, in the sexiest, skimpiest dress you've ever seen, and you feel and look fantastic. (Try to let go of other issues about dancers or dancing you might have, such as the "Omigod, strange men are about to see me naked" factor.) The club is packed—every table, couch, and bar stool is taken, so it's literally standing room only. Strippers (all friends of yours) are giving dances for men in the aisle walkways—because there's nowhere for them to sit. The music's pumping and the energy of the club is alive. There are so many people that you decide it'll just be easier to start at the beginning. You spot the man sitting closest to you and ask him if he wants a dance. He looks you up and down, thinks for a minute, and says, "No thanks," then looks away and resumes watching the stage. You collect yourself, move on to the man right next to him, and get another no. Now imagine that this happens to you one hundred times in a row. That you ask one hundred men if they want a dance from you, and every single one of the one hundred says no. How do you feel? Pretty crappy, right? It's kind of hard not to take it personally, because it feels awful!

Okay. Keep that awful feeling, and add one hundred *more* rejections to the ones you've already got. Now two hundred men have said no to you. Chances are that instead of insecure, you've started to just feel angry. Here you are, working your hardest and trying your best. What's wrong with these people? Okay, keep that anger, and add *another* one hundred rejections onto it. Now three hundred different men have all said no to you. Three hundred different men have politely told you that they'd rather not see you naked right now, thanks. At this point, after the three hundredth rejection, how do you imagine it feels? Kind of ridiculous, right? It moves to the level of the absurd. You can't take it personally, and you can't feel angry with the customers. At this point, you simply accept that all you can do is the best you can: keep your lip gloss fresh and keep pounding the floor. The night will end in either a bang or a bust (which it does for all dancers, once in a while) and you'll at least walk away knowing you've tried your hardest.

The point of the above mental exercise is to help you experience rejection as a dancer does. As you can see, it is hard not to take it personally—at first. This is why you, as civilian women, have a tendency to internalize it: because it happens so rarely. It's so upsetting that we want to understand why it happened and how we're to blame so we can prevent it from happening again. For dancers, though, the more rejection we experience, the more we externalize it. At some point it makes us angry, and at a further point we let it go. We hardly think about it anymore, because we know that no matter what, it's not us; it's *always* them.

~~~~~

So, as you see, the real secret to a stripper's sex appeal is her self-confidence. Men, the poor, daft creatures that they are, might think they are seeing the most toned, flawless woman in the world dance in front of them. But we know what they're really seeing is just a woman who is confident and comfortable with her body. As a nonstripper, you can increase your own self-confidence by spending more time naked—whether it's doing something silly like making a grocery list or just tucking in for the night. Then, when you get a chance, turn up the stereo as loud as you can to *dance!* Preferably naked, and as often as you can. Finally, join a team or some other competitive activity. It'll get you outside the house or office, help you make new friends, and increase your confidence as you learn and develop new skills. All of which will serve to strengthen your self-confidence.

Most importantly, learn the ten easy steps to the basic striptease. Whether you plan on surprising your man or not, every girl should know how to do one . . . just in case.

EXERCISE: THE STRIPTEASE

Every stripper has a basic dance she does for customers. Because each dancer has her own unique look, talent, and abilities, her dance is calculated to showcase her strengths and minimize her weaknesses. For example, some dancers are really flexible and like to flaunt it, while others are recovering from knee surgery and trying to move as little as possible. Learn the steps below, and change them to cater to your strengths. Maybe you have a terrific tush and want to show it off, or maybe it's your sexy shoulders and neck. Some girls just have a great sense of rhythm and are really good dancers. I'm not one of them, but I have mastered the really intense look (not unlike Derek Zoolander's "blue steel") and, having done some modeling, I pose pretty well.

(NOTE: This dance is designed to be given wearing a spandex dress and G-string—so try it in a slip or nightgown to get the same feeling.)

1. Turn on a song you love, one that makes you feel sexy.

2. Stand in the center of the room and dance for a few beats, while you really get into it.

3. Slowly reach down and pull up the hem of your dress, so that your G-string is exposed.

4. Lean forward and press your arms into your breasts, so that they are pushed up and outward, giving you maximum cleavage.

5. Teasingly pull down the top of your dress and pause for a few moments, giving your imaginary audience a chance to take all of you in. Then slide your dress all the way off and toss it aside.

6. Turn toward the right to give your eager audience a side angle.

7. Turn around and bend over, presenting your butt. Just flop on down, as if you are trying to touch your toes. You know you've got it right when you can feel the stretch in the back of your legs.

8. Come up and, keeping your back to the audience, shake your booty up and down the way girls in music videos do.

9. Turn toward the left, for another side angle.

10. Repeat steps 7 through 9 until the song is over.

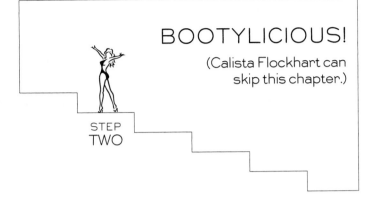

BOOTYLICIOUS!

(Calista Flockhart can
skip this chapter.)

STEP
TWO

In the November 2001 issue of Cosmopolitan, singer Beyoncé explained the inspiration behind her group Destiny's Child's 2001 hit song "Bootylicious." "When I gain weight, I tend to gain it on my hips and thighs. It's a common problem. Instead of feeling bad about it, I just say they're not ready for this jelly." For those of you who think a booty is something you knit for babies, and jelly something you spread on toast, let me enlighten you: "Booty" is your butt. Ass, can, keister, whatever. "Jelly" is the fat *on* your booty, ass, can, or keister. Bootylicious, then, is an adjective that describes 1) the pleasing appearance of a big, round backside, and 2) the pleasant feeling of having a big, round backside.

Now, although many of us are currently in the possession of a big, round backside, few, if any, of us are actually pleased by it. Which is why the song is so great. It tells us that the "problem" of having big hips and thighs isn't something we should stress over. And if anyone does have an issue with our tissue, it's because they're just not man enough to handle it. Let me add: right on! Although the song "Bootylicious" is about your butt, it's really the spirit and attitude . . . um, *behind* it that's important. After all, everybody's insecure about something—and strippers are no exception. The difference is that your insecurities hurt you emotionally, while a dancer's hurt where it really counts: financially. You see, strippers don't get paid to dance by the club. In fact, it's actually the opposite: We have to pay the club to dance. The amount varies depending on the club you're at and city you're in. In general, though, you can expect to pay more at clubs where the girls can reasonably expect to make more.

At some clubs, strippers can pay as much as two hundred dollars to the house on certain nights of the week, because of the high customer turnover. That's not including "tip out"—mandatory tips we give to certain people we work with, such as the DJ and the house mom. Depending on the service—such as the DJ's playing "Hot Blooded" every time you get up on stage to dance—you can expect to pay at least an extra fifty bucks to them too. Finally, you'll be tipping anyone else who may have helped you out over the course of the night, like a bouncer who tossed out an annoying customer or a floor host who hooked you up with a high roller. In all, it's the norm to pay an average of three hundred dollars a night to work there.

What does all of this mean? It means that when you are essentially paying three hundred dollars to walk in the door, you are going to make sure that you work damn hard to make money. Because the first fifteen (!) dances you do that night belong to the house. And if, for some ungodly reason, we don't make the house fee, we just owe the balance the next night. Which means that if we managed to pay only half our house fee on Thursday, we owe the house *four hundred and fifty dollars* on Friday. So it's not so much that we don't want to feel insecure as that we *can't afford* to feel insecure. You know the saying "If I had a dollar in my pocket for every time (fill in the blank here)?" Well, dancers don't get dollars put in their garters for every positive thought we have about ourselves, but in a very real way we do get dollars taken out of our garters for every negative thought. Being able to equate how secure we feel with how much money we make really helps us understand that our insecurities are ultimately our choice.

In this chapter, we'll talk about strippers' real bodies versus the media portrayal of them. Next, we'll look at the tragic affliction rampaging through strip clubs everywhere: tanorexia. We'll sail through the Bermuda Triangle of stripper angst: Boobs, Bloat, and Booty, and learn what we can do mentally and physically to handle our insecurities about them. We'll also go through some fun exercises and practical tips on how you at home can handle your own. Finally, I'll show you the most common and effective way dancers pump up a deflated ego—and how you can too. After all, being in the spotlight is hard, whether for an audience of one or one hundred. As every stripper knows, you don't need to lose your saddlebags or stretch marks; you just have to lose your insecurities about them. Because it's not enough to feel "secure" with your big ol' butt; you need to feel absolutely bootylicious!

REAL WOMEN, REAL BOOTIES

There are those who think that strip clubs propagate women's negative self-images by glorifying a body type that is an unattainable ideal. The people who think this have obviously never been to an actual strip club. As you learned in chapter 1, dancers are hot because they are in touch with their sexuality—not because they have "perfect" bods. To be fair, though, it is easy to see where the confusion comes from. Stripper chic is big right now, and lots of celebs rock the Stripperella look. First there are actual former strippers who have made "good." Courtney Love, *Baywatch* babe Donna D'Errico, and Anna Nicole Smith have all done their time on the pole. Then there are honorary strippers—celebrities who aren't dancers but whose work has mightily advanced the cause: Carmen Electra, Mariah Carey, Christina Aguilera, and Lil' Kim, to name a few.

Dancers are portrayed everywhere—in movies like *Striptease* and *Showgirls,* on television, in HBO's *The Sopranos* and on Spike TV's animated series *Stripperella* (voiced by Pamela Anderson); and, of course, in any Britney Spears video.

"Strippers" are even on the theatrical stage in the sold-out traveling revue *Pussycat Dolls,* whose famous emcees include Gwen Stefani, Christina Applegate, Charlize Theron, and Brittany Murphy.

The tricky part is that in all these instances, it's a famous actress (or singer) letting her inner stripper out. And in Hollywood, there are really only two body types: stick-thin with huge hooters or stick-thin without. Real strippers at real strip clubs don't have these proportions. And although dancers do make good money, we don't have the time, energy, or financial wherewithal to work out four hours a day—which is what Demi Moore reportedly did to get into shape for her role in *Striptease*—or maintain a 1,350-calories-a-day high-protein diet, which is part of *Alias* star Jennifer Garner's reported fitness regime.

Strippers, like real women, have five basic body types:

Athletic

Women with "athletic" bodies are slim, with a small bust and narrow hips. Model Rebecca Romijn-Stamos has a typical athletic body type, as does singer Pink, and actress Linda Evans (Krystle on *Dynasty* . . . the one with the shoulder pads).

Waif

You know the waif—she's the annoying one who after bearing four children still looks as skinny as a twelve-year-old boy. Calista Flockhart, Lara Flynn Boyle, Kate Moss, and all the "heroin chic" models fit into this category.

Top-Heavy

Some dancers are naturally top-heavy, born to have slim hips and large chests. Other dancers may or may not have the slim hips but have purchased the large chests to compensate. Every single Playboy Playmate fits into this category.

The Apple

Women with apple shapes can have large or small breasts and wide or narrow hips. What defines them as apple-shaped is their genetic predisposition to gaining weight around their stomach area. Comedienne Roseanne, Kelly Osbourne, and Rosie O'Donnell are three good examples of women with an apple shape.

Bottom-Heavy

Bottom-heavy women are categorized as having small breasts (in proportion to their backside), a narrow (or not so narrow) waist, and a large can in back. Jennifer Lopez is the most obvious example of someone fitting this body type.

Dancers, being human beings, all fit into one or another of these categories. Obviously, you will never walk into a strip club and see dancers who have Roseanne's proportions, but you will see dancers who will in thirty years' time (if they don't take care of themselves). The point is that all strippers have problem areas that are very difficult to conceal in one yard of sequined spandex. The need to find a way to eliminate these problem areas is what has led to the crippling stripper disease of tanorexia.

TANOREXIA

Tanorexia is an epidemic that has swept through strip clubs nationwide. It is characterized by women (and sometimes men . . . George Hamilton springs to mind) with deep, dark tans and somewhat leathery skin. Tanorexics who choose self-tans over suntans are known to have streaky, splotchy orange skin, with tinted palms and stained fingernails. However, because of the insidious nature of the disease, tanorexics are unable to see how tan they really are. When they look in the mirror, they mistakenly see pale, sallow, sickly winter skin. So they hit the tanning salon or self-tanner every day, never believing that they will ever be tan enough.

How did this horrible, disfiguring disease begin? No one knows for sure, but it seems likely that its origins lie at the heart of necessity. You see, a dark tan is a crucial component of the stripper look. A tan (and its corresponding tan lines) are to stripping what shoulder pads are to the power suit. They draw the eye upward, nip in the waist, and slim the look of the hips. A tan makes everyone look healthier, happier, and more fun to be around than they really are. And because the lighting at strip clubs is so dark, a tan also makes you look thinner. For that reason alone, a deep bronze tan is the most coveted accessory a stripper can own. If you're tan enough, you don't need to worry about stretch marks, belly bloat, or saddlebags. Tanning beds and tanning cream have the power to magically blend away cellulite the way no thigh cream or Endermologie procedure can.

Besides making you look thinner, tans are also incredibly sexy. They evoke the memory of long summer days, running around without any clothes on, and dashing through sprinklers or the sea spray at the beach. Anyone who determinedly remains pale looks like they've never had a day of fun in their lives. Of course, there are always those who take it to the extreme. By wanting to look too tan, too thin, or too sexy, they end up tanning their skin the color of my cherry-stained oak-wood cabinets (à la Donatella Versace).

Although tanorexia does not seem to have any negative impact on dancers while they are at work, it does severely effect their social lives. For example, they are always fending off strangers who ask them where they just got back from vacation. Dancers are then forced to either make something up—"Uh, Aruba?"—or to admit the embarrassing truth: that they didn't get back from vacation, they really just got back from the tanning salon. A tanorexic self-tanner's social life suffers even worse. Because of the way fake tans look as they slough off your skin (think molting snake), strangers (especially hot men) may avoid a self-tanorexic completely, afraid of catching her apparent skin condition.

Still, there is hope. Advances in topical self-tanners will eventually eliminate the crusty-orange color your skin turns when you use too much product. In addition, Australia and Europe are running clinical trials on a self-tanning pill that increases the natural melanin production in your skin, resulting in a deep, dark tan from the inside out.

Sadly, there will probably never be a safe way to tan your skin at the beach or at a salon. Even tanning beds that have UVA and UVB filters damage your skin to some degree. But as awareness grows and new technology develops, there is every expectation that tanning-salon tanorexics will make the switch to safer self-tans. And so, while a true tanorexic may never believe she is tan enough, at least she won't die trying.

Let's now move on to the unholy trinity of stripper insecurity: Boobs, Bloat, and Booty.

BOOBS

We Must Increase Our Bust!

Okay, here it is. Let's have a frank discussion about strippers and implants. As I see it, the biggest problem we are currently facing in our society is that our technology has outpaced—no, *blown past*—our ability to assimilate it into our moral code. Back in the bad old days, you had to take what you were given. If you were born ugly, you died ugly. This is no longer the case. Now that plastic surgery is relatively cheap, easy, and, in most cases, safe, people are debating whether it's morally correct to get it. These are the same people who think that it's wrong to be happy but supernoble to suffer. Unfortunately, the truth is that unnecessary suffering isn't noble—it just sucks. So here is my position: If something is causing you emotional pain or stress, fix it. There's no point in living with something that's bothering you, because the psychological stress is easily as harmful as the surgical stress.

That said, there are lots and lots of bad reasons to get plastic surgery. Half of all dancers are what we in the industry call "natural," meaning they don't have implants. They might have had their eyes or noses done, with a couple of rounds of lipo to top it all off, but without the implants, they are still considered to be "natural." Many natural girls decide to get implants because they think that they'll make more money. I know, because I was one of them. I started out dancing with rather nice, small B-cups. I looked good, I felt good, and I was making good money. Then, for whatever reason—the economy, the stock market, PMS—I decided that I wasn't making *enough* money. I stared in envy at all the girls with implants, like the only tweenie in the locker room who hasn't started to develop yet. I became convinced that I wasn't making money because my boobs weren't big enough. So I took what money I did have and bought myself a pair. The moral of this story is exactly what you think it's going to be: I didn't make a dime more money with implants then I did without. The reason is that men love all boobs. Natural, fake, big, medium, or small—every customer loves them all. (Sorry, I couldn't resist the rhyme.) So while one man might like double-D's, he'll still buy a dance from a double-A girl, because the truth is, what he really likes best is the variety.

Another bad reason to get surgery is because you have an unrealistic idea of what the end result will be. This is like a way more serious version of thinking you'll look just like Cindy Crawford if you get your hair cut the same way. But any hairdresser or surgeon worth his salt will tell you that this is definitely not the case.

Most natural girls have breasts that are B-cups or under. In addition, most of these natural girls aren't twenty-two years old with perky little nubs that have never felt the insistent pull of gravity. They have some hang, some sag, and some flatness. In fact, even women with implants have hang, sag, and flatness. Which is why dancers are forever wondering whether their boobs are big enough. They mistakenly think that an increase in size will make up for whatever it is that they don't like about their breasts. They get implants (or bigger ones) because they think their boobs will look better. And they do—inside their spandex. But take the top down, and you frequently see some surgical abnormalities that you wouldn't wish on your worst enemy. Here they are:

THE UNIBOOB—A uniboob arises when two implants have been positioned so close together, they indeed do look like one solid breast. The uniboob usually results when implants that are too big are placed inside a girl whose skin is too tight.

ROCKS 'N' SOCKS—This happens when the implants are too small, placed inside a girl whose skin is too loose. It can also happen when someone goes through a major weight change, through pregnancy, for example. The breast skin stretches, leaving the implants dangling—resulting in the unfortunate look of someone carrying rocks around in a pair of old tube socks.

ENFORCED CLEAVAGE—This, like the uniboob, occurs when the skin is too tight. To compensate, doctors sometimes try to give the breasts a natural look by placing them close enough together to form a crease of "cleavage" between them. This might not sound bad—but try to imagine a whole loaf of bread with one narrow slice across the center, and you'll get the picture.

OPPOSING NIPPLES—Sometimes, because of poor placement, the impants will force the nipples in opposite directions. I actually worked with a woman whose left nipple faced north-northeast while her right nipple faced south-southwest. Another woman's implants sat so low in her chest that both nipples pointed straight up—toward the North Pole.

THE LANDSLIDE—This occurs when the skin around implants that have been placed under the muscle suddenly stretches—like with rocks 'n' socks. This stretching causes the nipples, and the skin around them, to sag off the implant, looking a bit like a hiker dangling from a cliff.

Even when the implants are placed perfectly and everything looks great, there are still other things to worry about. For example, every single woman with implants will experience rippling. Ripples are—well, quite literally, ripples. The saline, silicone, or other liquid sloshes around inside your implant as you move, causing tiny waves under the surface of your skin. This is a little less obvious in certain types of implants, but because of the ocean motion, you will never be able to fool anyone into thinking your breasts are real. Of course, rippling is an aesthetic concern, not a health problem. There are more serious risks involved with breast implants, so if you are considering implants, you need to thoroughly consult with your doctor first.

Since bigger is definitely not always better. I would also recommend watching at least one episode of *Nip/Tuck* on FX and then asking yourself the following questions: Are you disfigured? Did you have some kind of procedure or biopsy that could be remedied by surgery? Or are your boobs markedly different sizes? Have you born and breast-fed more than six children? Did you used to be a man? Unless you are desperately unhappy with your breasts, you are probably better off without surgery.

In the meantime, here are some practical tips to give your bust a boost:

- Turn on your high beams! Sure, huge hooters always get noticed. But nothing draws a man's eye (and the rest of him) over to you more effectively than hard nips. Why? Not because you look like you're cold— rather, it's because you look hot. The two primary times women are at attention are when they're standing in a meat locker and during foreplay. If you look like you're already halfway to happy, all men will want to do is escort you the rest of the trip.

   (Note: You can actually purchase nipple inserts, called Bodyperks, for your bra if you want to look, um, alert but don't want to hire a nipple tweaker, or bother having to rub ice on yourself to "wake up.")

- Pretend you're back in junior high and do the "We must, we must, we must increase our bust!" exercises. They actually do work, by building up the pectoral muscle underneath your breasts. The bigger your muscles, the bigger, higher, and firmer your boobs will look.

EXERCISE: WELL-ROUNDED DEVELOPMENT

(The one girl who got boobs in fifth grade can skip this exercise.)

Remember in grade school or junior high when you first started to "develop"? Getting boobs was new and exciting, and you were proud of your little nubs. Maybe you even forced your mom out bra shopping to get something to support your triple-A's. You might have even stuck a little toilet paper or some socks in there to pick up the slack. Or at least I did. So let's go back for a minute. Try to feel as proud of your boobs as you did when you first got them. Stand up straight, roll your shoulders back, and stick your chest out as far as it will go. (You remember; it's how Heather, the popular girl, used to stand.) Then just do the stuff you'd normally do. Try to walk around in private (or in public, if you're feeling adventurous) with your rack on display for as long as you can. Strippers know that the more attention they pay to a certain area of their bodies, the more attention men will pay to that area. Similarly, the more you like and appreciate an area of your body, the more men will like and appreciate that area too. So stick 'em out!

BLOAT

Deep Rising

We all know the feeling. We wake up one morning, our tongues a little dry and our heads a little achy. We're not hungover, but the early-morning light hurts our eyes as if we'd been out all night on a tequila bender. The hot shower and even hotter coffee help a little, but it all takes a predicted and ugly turn for the worst getting dressed, when we realize that we can't close the button on our slacks. We've stuck to our diet and have been exercising regularly (or not—whatever), so we know exactly what's to blame for this discouraging turn of events. Bloat. Even the word sounds awful . . . *bloat.* Say it out loud. Go ahead. No one will think you're crazy. Bloat. You might even get a little bit of sympathy. Bloat. Bloat. *Bloat bloat bloat.*

So what is bloat? And why does it happen to us? My friend Rachel, an RN who put her hard-earned dancing dollars to use paying for nursing school, says that the primary cause of bloat is water retention, which comes from changes in your monthly cycle, high-sodium diets, alcohol consumption, and . . . inappropriate antidiuretic-secreting tumors.

Bloat (and all of its causes) is the number one enemy of dancers everywhere. First, it's hard to dance when you're feeling bloated, because of the lethargy it causes. When you feel bloated, you just feel tired. And since dancing involves the hard physical activity of, well, dancing, you just get exhausted.

The second problem with being bloated is that you not only feel bloated, you look bloated. Now, here's a little dancers' secret: We don't all have taut, toned, sexy six-pack tummies. In fact, you'd be surprised at how many dancers not only don't do crunches but don't do any other form of exercise either. The truth is that with dancing, the hours are so crazy and the job so physically grueling (we're in our five-inch heels eight hours a night, four nights a week) that we're usually too exhausted to drag our tired heinies to the gym. To get our tight-looking tummies, we rely on a tried-and-true combination of bronzing powder (see chapter

3) and lung power. Lung power? you ask. Why, yes. Most dancers rely heavily on the power of their windpipes to suck in their stomachs to a concave arc. You might not think it's possible, but the next time you're near a mirror, try it. It doesn't matter what you weigh or how big a potbelly you have. Find a full-length mirror and stand sideways. Pull yourself up and stand as tall as you can. Lift your rib cage and arch your upper back slightly, so that it has a feeling of opening up. Exhale completely, without losing your posture, and then slowly breathe in. As you breath in, contract your abdominal muscles as hard as you can. Suck! suck! suck those muscles in, visualizing your belly button actually touching your spinal column. Hold your breath and your stomach in this position and look at yourself in the mirror. Chances are you'll be amazed at how far you can suck your stomach in, and how flat and toned your abs look when you do. From this position, with a little concentration and a little practice, you can probably lift your rib cage higher and suck your tummy in even farther. You've probably also noticed how uncomfortable and contorted you feel. Well, that's how dancers feel pretty much all the time. We could work out, I guess, but, like you, we don't really want to. Unfortunately, monthly bloat is the perfect foil for our best-laid stripper tricks. If, for example, you did try the above exercise while going through some bloat, you'll see that no matter how forceful your lungs or your will, it's impossible to suck in your tummy when you're bloated. Which, of course, makes it harder to feel confident when you're wearing only some strategically placed sparkles.

I once had to work a bachelor party when I was retaining so much water I thought I was going to pop. All I could think about was my stretched-out gut and how unsexy I felt. Instead of feeling embarrassed by it, I decided on a whim to *work* the bloat.

I mean, I couldn't suck it in, so I pushed it out instead. Like a mantra, I chanted, "Bloat, bloat, bloat" as I made my way toward the men ogling me from their chairs. And as I laughed at myself and my silliness, all the men saw was a confident girl enjoying her body. They ate it up! I could do no wrong, and my stomach and I made a lot of money that night.

At the club, when we're feeling particularly fat or bloated or both, there are a couple of tricks we use to cover it up. The first thing we do at the beginning signs of bloat buildup is put on a garter belt. Garter belts are fantastic for hiding a thickening waist or a bloated belly. If for whatever reason we don't have one to hide behind, we can adjust our dance to highlight the areas of our body that we do feel confident about. For example, instead of taking our dress completely off while giving a dance, we might take the top down and hoist the bottom up, leaving the dress gathered around our middle. This sounds like it might look strange, but it actually looks kind of sexy. Keep in mind that these are tight spandex dresses we're climbing in and out of—not big baggy muumuus. Finally, if we're not comfortable wearing a garter belt or keeping our dress around our tummies, another way to camouflage the bloat is to dance really close to the customer so that all the proportions are skewed. If all he can see is your left breast, he can't tell that your ass is huge.

- If you are suffering from excess bloat, there is no need for it to stop you from feeling terrifically sexy, or having terrific sex, for that matter. Dress up for sex in garters (see chapter 4 for tips on what to wear) or leave everything on instead. It'll make him think you're so hot for him you can't waste time taking your clothes off.
- If you're not going to be naked, bust out the girdle.

Having something else suck you in so you don't have to will help, as will the cute little outfit you put on over it. You'll be able to look at your reflection and truthfully think, "Hey! I feel awful, but I look really good!"

STRIPPER TIPS!

If you find that you are bloated, whether it's because you are expecting your monthly visitor or not, you need to drink *a lot* of water. Your body retains water only when you're not getting enough of it. Again, dehydration, too much salt, alcohol, and caffeine are common culprits. So try to cut down on the Bud and beer nuts.

Another source of bloat is constipation. Irregularity and the gas and other unpleasantries that come with it are frequent sources of bloating. Many dancers swear by eating one bowl of Fiber One or other high-fiber cereal before going to bed. You'll be less bloated, become "regular," and do all your farting in the middle of the night, when no one else will be awake to notice it.

Tide's Out

Sometimes saying that you're bloated is really just a euphemistic way of saying that you're fat. It's nicer and less stressful to tell yourself that you've gained five pounds of water weight than to admit it's really Nacho Cheesier Doritos and Chunky Monkey weight. For some fortunate souls out there, the problem is the exact opposite: They lack bloat. Or, rather, the curves that a few extra pounds of whatever kind of weight gives you. For dancers, like regular women, this isn't much of a problem. I can think of only two women over the course of my dancing history who were actually Lara Flynn thin. The reason is that while superthin women like Kate Moss or Victoria Beckham (Posh Spice) might look good on the fashion-show runway, they'd look awful on a strip-club runway. Jutting ribs and hipbones might look cool coming out of a pair of low-rise jeans, but they look scary coming out of a G-string.

STRIPPER TIPS!

If you find that you do lack curves . . . gain some weight, for God's sake! And hook up with a personal trainer at the gym. A dancer friend of mine from Finland who was tragically born without any butt at all sculpted herself a nice little keister at the gym with the help of a personal trainer. By building up certain muscles, the pecs and glutes for example, you can sculpt yourself some brand-new curves.

Or you could go the opposite route and flaunt it. Wear platforms to look taller, and practice pouting and looking bored. Everyone will think you're a model!

EXERCISE: I'M TOO SEXY FOR MY . . . FAT

Most of time, we talk about feeling fat like it's a bad thing. We'll whine, moan, and complain to our friends about how gelatinous we feel because nothing fits. The next time you feel the urge to grumble about how large you are, do this instead: In your deep-est, sultriest voice, say out loud, "I am soooo fat." Say it as though you were describing a delicious entrée or dessert—"Drizzled with rich, creamy, warm milk chocolate." Now try it again, and finish the thought. "I am soooo huge, I can't even zip up my fat pants." Then sensuously lick your lips and bat your eyelashes. Say it over and over in the sexiest, scratchiest phone-sex-operator voice you can muster. Repeat, as necessary, until you no longer care how fat you feel.

BOOTY

Days of Thunder ... Thighs

One of the most vexing areas of a woman's body is, of course, her butt. As far as body parts go, butts are really important. They pro-vide crucial padding and lumbar support. They cushion painful falls and act as a fat reserve in case we ever find ourselves stranded on a desert island. Still, the butt is a rather ornery body part; it refuses to be a team player and instead insists on playing by its own rules. For example, no matter how many times you tell your butt that you live in an area where food and water are plen-tiful, your butt will steadfastly refuse to lessen its fat reserve. No, rationalization has absolutely no impact on your butt's size, and it seems sometimes that proper diet and exercise don't really have an impact on your butt's size either.

Which is why after surviving the 1980s, with the emergence of the "supermodel," and the early '90s, with "heroin chic," it's really exciting that bigger women with real-life bodies are coming into their own. And, of course, the one woman responsible for this sea change in booty awareness is (duh) Jennifer Lopez. Love her or hate her, nobody has done more to promote the real-life sexiness of a real-life woman's body. Jennifer Lopez has the classic pear shape of most women—small breasts, thick waist, with a large butt and thighs. Sure, she works out at least a couple of hours a day, to keep her pear shape tight, but at least she hasn't resorted to getting implants or surgery to fit into the more idealized hourglass mold. She's beautiful and unflinchingly sexy, in the body God gave her. If for nothing else, she's a great role model for having confidence in yourself, no matter what your body type.

I actually remember when this change occurred. It was back in the mid-'90s, when Cindy Crawford was still the "it" model and was hosting the MTV show *House of Style.* She was asked (God only knows why) to comment on then–rising star Lopez's butt. Cindy very diplomatically said something along the lines of how she could never feel confident having a butt that big, but she thought it was great that Lopez could. Now, any way you slice it, Cindy was saying that Jennifer's ass was just too damn big. It's amazing that now it's "okay" to have a big butt, à la Lopez, and that not so long ago, it wasn't. Most of us are still living in a place within ourselves where having a big butt (and I include thighs in my definition of butt as well) is definitely not okay. Because we don't have the team of personal trainers, stylists, and hot men willing to marry us that J.Lo does, it's a lot harder to feel as if we're at our best. Even most dancers, who by necessity of the job need to come to peace with their posteriors, have trouble feeling bootylicous. Here's an especially awful incident that happened to me:

One night I went to the VIP room with a lovely Brazilian gentleman, here in the States on business. We had ordered champagne and chatted for a bit, and after a while, I stood up to dance for him.

I had gotten no more than three minutes into my dance when he suddenly grabbed the saddlebags on both my thighs and firmly squeezed them, declaring, "I love this! You have . . . what do you call it? *Cellulite* in all the right places!" I stopped dead in my dance, stunned. Now, you know I had spent about fifteen minutes in the mirror that evening, looking at my saddlebags from every angle. And you know that I had poked them, with a disgusted look on my face, and covered them with my hands to see how slammin' my body would look without them. And you know that I'd spent an additional fifteen minutes psyching myself up by telling myself things like "You only notice them because you don't like them—nobody else even sees them" and "They're really not that bad. They look fine!" And then suddenly—*ouch!*—came the crushing realization that not only were my thighs so big that a customer felt compelled to comment on them; he had to grab them and shake them too! After the shock wore off, I realized that I had two choices: I could have the bouncer forcibly remove the gentleman, and drown my sorrows in the last of the champagne, or I could accept the fact that I was actually pretty lucky. I mean, yeah, I had a big butt, but I also had someone who was happy to pay me four hundred dollars an hour to see it! How many other people can say that?

For dancers, there are a couple of ways to camouflage a keister. The first thing we'll do is apply lots and lots of a dark-toned self-tanner on our butts and thighs. Then, after the color has developed, we'll put a layer of bronzing powder on top of it. As you've seen, the darker the tan, the skinnier you look, so we're very liberal in our application. (See chapter 3 for more self-tanner tips.) Another thing dancers will do while giving a dance is to leave the dress around her hips, instead of around her middle like she'd do if she felt bloated.

- At home, you can try leaving just a skirt on for sex. Miniskirts—or anything tight and short—cover the questionable area and are still sexy.
- Another great way to hide a big ol' butt is to wear a boy-cut thong. (See chapter 4 for details.)
- Again, if you know you aren't going to be seen naked by anyone, wear a pair of control-top panty hose or a foundation garment under your outfit. It'll slim and smooth you out. You'll look better, and feel more confident too.

Practically, there isn't a lot you can do to reduce the size of your butt or thighs, except a balanced diet and exercise. A personal trainer can put you on the right track to reducing your overall body-fat percentage, which will therefore reduce the size of your can. After you get going on a practical program, rent a bunch of J.Lo videos and relax.

EXERCISE: WORK THOSE SQUAREPANTS!

The next time you're feeling self-conscious because your hips are too wide or your thighs rub together, imagine that you are a dancer at a club. Cross the room to your man imagining your hips (or stomach or thighs) wider then they really are, taking up doorways and knocking things over. Slam them to the left and slam them to the right! Knock over a skinny little cocktail waitress, or the lamp on your nightstand! The question now is not whether they're too big, but is he man enough to handle them?

Days of Thunder ... Thighs (or Not)

One of the funniest scenes in the first *Charlie's Angels* movie is when Cameron Diaz is asked to dance onstage at a filming of a *Soul Train* episode. With absolute glee she jumps up onstage, ready and willing to dance to any song that comes on. The music cues up, and to everyone's delight it's the classic Sir Mix-A-Lot song "Baby Got Back." Diaz shakes, jumps, and twists with joyful abandon as the stunned audience looks on. We, the moviegoers, are left in our seats, laughing so hard that popcorn threatens to come out of our noses. What makes this scene so funny? It's not Diaz's ability to dance like a total spaz—although that, of course, is part of it. No, we're laughing because she's a skinny white girl dancing to a song about big, shapely women. We're laughing because it's a song about big asses and Cameron Diaz (I'm sorry, Cam) *HAS NO ASS!* We're laughing at Cameron Diaz because she has nothing to back that thing up. No junk in the trunk. Isn't this some miracle of modern moviegoing that there is actually a scene where we are able to laugh at the tall, gorgeous, rail-thin blonde on screen because she's not fat enough? I'm certainly sorry to offend any woman who is self-conscious because she was born without a booty—but there are so few of you out there, I'm sure you'll understand and take this in fun, the way it is meant. On another, very real level, what makes this scene great is that although Cameron Diaz doesn't, as discussed, have anything resembling an ass, she is unafraid and unapologetic about getting up onstage and shaking what she does have. This is important, because it goes to the heart of stripper self-confidence. It doesn't matter what you have to work with, it's how well you work it.

~~~~~~

So there you have it: dancers' biggest problem areas and how we deal with them. However, the most important weapon we have in our arsenal of self-esteem is the ability to externalize our insecurities.

When our egos are deflated, we find a way to pump them up!

The best remedy for feeling in a funk is to take to your bed with a pint of ice cream and a bag of Chee-tos. And, of course, junkfood therapy isn't effective unless you grab your remote and watch an all-day *Trading Spaces* marathon. Unfortunately for most of us, this isn't really an option. If you work a regular job and try it, you could get fired. If you're a full-time mom, your kids will have already eaten all the junk food. Either way, all you have left is your own ability to find a creative way to pull yourself out of your funk.

In any situation where we don't feel good about ourselves, we use whatever is at our disposal to help us feel better—and I'm not talking about tequila shots, either. For some people, it might be xeroxing copies of your naked butt, or frittering away company time by looking for a pair of gently worn Prada heels on eBay. For dancers, the most useful tool at our disposal is . . . the DJ.

GONNA FLY NOW

Most strip clubs have one big, centrally located stage, with a few smaller ones scattered throughout the establishment. The largest stage is usually called the main stage, and the smaller stages are called something silly, like the "diamond stage," as opposed to the "side door next to the dumpster stage." Every stripper is on rotation, meaning that she'll have to dance on each of the club's stages at least two or three times each night. Dancing on the side stages can be a bit of a drag, because they're usually so out of the way that it's impossible to make crucial eye contact with customers. But dancing on the main stage is just about the greatest thing in the world.

It doesn't matter how tired, cranky, or bloated you feel . . . it's well known that the power of song can perk you up. Like when you're driving along the highway and some road-raging SUV comes roaring up behind you, passes, and then cuts you off? And just as you're unwisely about to step on the gas to give him a dose of his own medicine, Toni Basil's "Mickey" comes on the radio, and suddenly everything's okay again. Similarly, any civilian with stripper fantasies can well imagine the incredible rush you get stepping onto the stage with the lights pulsing as the opening strains of "Start Me Up" by the Rolling Stones kicks in. You know how it goes—first the guitar, then the drums. Then Mick comes in. You start feeling it: the music, Mick's voice, and then suddenly the song is about you. You dance onstage, under the hot, blinding lights, and he's begging you, Mick Jagger is begging you, every man in the audience is begging you not to let a grown man cry. You make a grown man cry. You make a dead man come.

The first song of a stage set is the dancer's way of introducing herself to the audience and telling them a little about herself, other than, of course, what her measurements are. Since the music you dance to can make or break a stage set, it's no surprise that strippers are notoriously possessive of "their" songs. You can usually tell which dancer is up on the main stage by whatever the DJ is playing at that moment.

The obvious choices for strippers are songs like AC/DC's "You Shook Me All Night Long," with its lyrics about a sexy, powerful woman, or even Blondie's "One Way or Another"—a great way to let the audience know that "I'm gonna gitcha gitcha gitcha gitcha." Some girls like to think outside the box, so to speak, so they'll choose atypical fare that represents them more personally. For example, one of the hottest women at the New York gentlemens's club Scores usually opened her stage set with Pearl Jam's somber "Alive." Another dancer opened with Madonna's "Hanky Panky" . . . you remember . . . *nothing like a good spanky.* And yet another girl favored only country-western music, so the DJ had to remember not to put her up before or after the girls who liked rap or metal.

In some way, all of us use music. Strippers have their stage sets. On the TV show *Ally McBeal,* the character John Cage had a theme song that ran through his head at crucial moments—good and bad—in his life to give him support and inspiration. Ally McBeal had the Pips to back her up in times of crisis. You should too.

Here are my personal recommendations. I would be remiss in naming this chapter after the song "Bootylicious" and not exploring with you why this is such a fantastic song. Since the deep, deep wisdom of it has been lost (partially because you can't understand what they're singing), here are the key lyrics to know and own: "I don't think you're ready for this jelly / Cause my body too bootylicious for you, babe."

I recommend playing "Bootylicious," as loud as you can, preferably naked, while dancing wildly in the mirror. It's important to do this regularly, but especially when you are feeling like even you are not ready to handle all that jelly. This attitude works for every other flaw you have too. Ignoring them will make you crazy (take it from one who knows), but embrace them and there's no stopping the money or the adoration of your fans.

Another fantastic song to pick you up is "Baby Got Back" by Sir Mix-A-Lot. I need to get my gangsta on and give a shout-out to Sir Mix-A-Lot. It's the first, the original, and the best homage to women everywhere with more junk in the trunk than they know what to do with. I'm still amazed that any woman could possibly be offended by it. I think those who are haven't really listened to the lyrics, and just dismiss it with "Oh, I hate this song—it's all about how much he likes big asses." Well, okay, yes, that's true. He does like big butts. But isn't that a good thing? I mean, since that's what most of us have? For those of you who have never really had an opportunity to appreciate Sir-Mix-A-Lot's opus, here are the most important lyrics to know: "My anaconda don't want none unless you got buns, hon." For those of you new to the world of hip-hop, this sentence can be roughly translated as meaning: No thank you, miss. I would rather not have sexual relations with you if you do not have a big butt. Good day.

Now, "Bootylicious" and "Baby Got Back" fall into the R&B and hip-hop genres of music, respectively. For those of you who remain firmly unconverted to hip-hop, there is a great rock song, appropriately titled "Fat Bottomed Girls," by Queen that covers the same subject matter.

If you ignore the first verse—something about a "naughty nanny" making a big man out him—you'll find an awesome tribute to big women everywhere: "Oh, are you gonna let it all hang out / Fat bottomed girls you make the rockin' world go round."

The central theme in these three songs is letting it all hang out, which is really only something a bigger woman can do, because skinny chicks have nothing to let hang. However, as I've mentioned, not every woman has a big ol' butt (or stomach or whatever). Unfortunately, there really aren't any songs that deal with any of the other issues that women are insecure about. For example, there are no songs that glorify flat chests, forehead wrinkles, or fatty arms. In these cases, it's best to just replace the lyrics; i.e., "Flat Bottomed Girls," and sing along. Clever, huh?

Of course, these songs are also talking about inhibitions. It's about feeling free, wild, and unstoppable. It's about liking sex so much that you don't care that your belly is slapping up against your man's (or your own) chin. This is an important truth! You don't care what you look like while riding a roller coaster, so you shouldn't care what you look like while riding your man.

When their favorite song comes on, strippers explode onto the stage in a flurry of sequins, sex, and sass to give their audience a performance they'll never forget. You should give your man the same.

EXERCISE: THE OVERTURE

You will need: a copy of your theme song and something to play it on.

While you're going through your normal presex preparations (showering, shaving, birth control, etc.) play your theme song as loud as you can. If your man is in the house, wear a Walkman so he can't hear it. Allow yourself to get lost in the song until you really feel that *you're* the one who's bootylicious, *you're* the baby with the back, *you're* the one who makes the rockin' world go round. Play it over and over until you're ready to get out there and rock your man's world.

Other songs to give a listen to are:

"Man! I Feel Like a Woman" by Shania Twain

"Brick House" by the Commodores

"Can't Get Enough of Your Love, Babe" by Barry White

"Call Me" by Blondie

You get the theme here. Choose whatever songs of whatever genres work for you. Just be careful—sometimes songs can have an effect opposite of the one intended. For example, while I personally love dancing onstage to Queen's "Fat Bottomed Girls," I knew a dancer who burst into tears and ran off the stage sobbing when the DJ played it for her. Music should make you feel better, not worse.

ACCEPTANCE

The final step in the process of becoming bootylicious is acceptance. From time to time both strippers and civilians come up against insecurities that can be both painful and costly. When dancers are feeling fat, bloated, or ugly, they have two choices: to waste their house fee by sitting in the dressing room feeling sorry for themselves, or to accept the fact that they're not at their best and try to make some money anyway. To do this, dancers first have to identify what's bothering them. Some dancers might feel insecure because they've gained weight; others might just be a having bad-hair day. Whatever the issue is, it's then up to the dancer to come up with a practical strategy to combat it. This might mean wearing a garter belt on her more bloated days, or slicking her hair back if she can't combat the frizz.

Finally, after she's taken whatever steps are necessary to feel more confident, it's time for the stripper to let it go. This means accepting that she feels insecure and recognizing that wherever she is, it's the best it's going to get right now. This is important! Once you stop looking at your flaws and trying to fix them, you'll see that you actually look pretty great the way you are.

GLAMA SLAMA

STEP
THREE

Not everyone is lucky enough to be blessed with Halle's beauty or J.Lo's complexion. The truth is that great beauties are rare, and that most of the women who seem beautiful in the media are really quite average stripped of their makeup and stylists. Even Britney Spears is not beautiful in the classical sense of the word. The reason behind Britney's enduring popularity is that there is a difference between beauty and hotness. Not every woman can be beautiful, but every woman can look hot. Katie Couric got some highlights and went from mousy to hot. Jennifer Aniston got a haircut and went from cute to Mrs. Brad Pitt. Alyssa Milano got hot by going from bad-girl B-movie actress (*Embrace of the Vampire* and *Poison Ivy 2,* anyone?) to *cleaning up* her image for prime-time TV. And it's hotness, not beauty, that the stripper sells.

A stripper presents a total package to the audience. Hair, nails, and makeup are always flawlessly done. A dancer doesn't do this because she wants to please or turn men on; she does this because it turns *her* on. You see, hotness isn't caring about your looks—it's *taking care* of them. When you look the best you possibly can, you feel powerful and good about yourself. And feeling powerful and good about yourself is what makes you hot.

In real life, however, it can be almost impossible to find time to take care of the things you need to, let alone want to. I remember standing in the dressing room of the club where I work and realizing I had gone the whole day without brushing my teeth. I had been so busy doing mommy stuff that I had completely forgotten to worry about basic oral hygiene. It was only after I made a conscious decision to limit my fluid intake so I could save time by peeing less that I realized I had a serious problem with time management. If, like me, you find yourself pressed for time to get the simplest things done, you need to reprioritize. Caring for yourself needs to be made a necessity in your life, not something you get around to after cleaning the oven or sending the fax out. You see, budgeting in the time to be hot is the most important step in your transformation.

In this chapter you may come across beauty tips that seem too in-depth or time-consuming to work into a real-life schedule. However, in the exercise section at the end of this chapter, you'll find ways to sneak in an extra few minutes a day, which, pooled together, are all you will need to maintain a more glam look.

LET'S GO, GIRLS

Pamela Anderson is not a stripper, but she is the industry-wide standard on how to look if you are. Pam's unapologetic, full-on glamour-girl, in-your-face hotness is the look to which all starlets, strippers, and centerfolds aspire. Like Barbie's, Pam's look is universal. Tia Carrere, Janet Jackson, even Shakira have all done their own versions. In "Part I: Makeup," I will give you the tips and tricks that dancers use, to get this look at home.

The makeup products you will need are: foundation, concealer, and powder in your skin tone; black or brown eyeliner; eyeshadow in frosty white or beige *and* in black or brown; lengthening mascara in black or brown; blush in a honey or toasty brown color, and/or bronzing powder; lip liner in deep nude; lipstick in a pearly pink or peach; and clear lip gloss. Since you probably already own most of these products and know how to use them, we'll go through some others that you might not be familiar with. These are false eyelashes, semipermanent lipstick, and BeneFit Cosmetics' SheLaq. Finally, at the end of this section, I will take you through a step-by-step guide to applying makeup to get the Glama Pam look.

PART I: MAKEUP

False Eyelashes

To the layperson, false eyelashes are necessary only if you are 1) a drag-queen or 2) J.Lo. In reality, it would be hard to find an actress or model who isn't wearing false eyelashes. You don't think those lush, full lashes in mascara ads are real, do you? False eyelashes make everyone's eyes look beautiful. They are about a thousand times more effective than an eyelash curler and mascara combined. And if you only apply a few, the effect will be subtle but gorgeous. Falsies come in a variety of styles, but the best bet for a natural look are the tiny individual lashes that you just glue on where you need them. You can also get it done for you at many salons—they're called eyelash extensions, and this is the safest, easiest way to do it. It costs about fifty bucks and they last for around two weeks. Look in your local phone book for full-service beauty salons, then call around and ask if it's something they do. However, if you're hell-bent on doing it yourself, follow the directions below.

TO APPLY

Individual lashes come in small trays, with about seventy-five tiny lash clumps to a tray. To apply individual lashes, you will need tweezers and eyelash glue. Using the tweezers, remove the lash that you want to apply from the tray. Apply a tiny drop of glue to the base of the lash. Wait twenty seconds for the glue to become tacky. Place the false lash over your own lash, as close to the base of your eyelid as possible, pressing the glue into your lash with the tweezers. Hold it here for about five seconds to set the lash, and tada! Long, natural-looking lashes! Repeat as necessary to fill in your lash line. Generally, two to four lashes per eye ought to do it.

IMPORTANT NOTE: Needless to say, *tweezers, glue, and eyeballs are a dangerous combination, so be careful!*

Lipstick

Guys are into full-looking lips—that's why we went through that phase in the early nineties where everyone wore superdark lip liner with superlight lipstick. Well, strippers *still* rock this look. The classic stripper lip is dark liner placed well outside of the natural lip line, filled in with a light frosty gloss on the lip. Unfortunately, even long-lasting liner tends to slide off and end up all over your face, especially if you are eating, drinking, or making out. Happily, there's a new lipstick technology on the market that uses semipermanent color and stays on for hours.

Revlon, Cover Girl, and Max Factor all make versions, but my favorite is Max Factor's Lipfinity. The texture is a viscous liquid that dries in a layer. The more coats you apply, the thicker the layer. Use this in place of lip liner to build up the area just outside your natural lip line, so it is flush with your lip. This way, there is no obvious contrast between where your lip ends and your lip liner begins. To use, first put a thin layer of color all over your lips. Next, use an old lip brush to apply a few layers just outside your natural lip line to build up your upper (or lower) lip. This changes the visual place where your skin ends and your lip begins. Allow about five minutes for it to dry, then set it with a light dusting of loose powder. Then apply a long-lasting lip liner over your new lip line. (You can also use a semipermanent lipstick in a darker shade to line your lips after you've built them up.) Top this with a coat of BeneFit's SheLaq, which is basically shellac for makeup. Let it dry, and then pop on a coat of shimmery gloss (it's usually included in the package with the lipstick). Bam! You will have natural-looking, full lips that stay put all night.

STRIPPER TIPS!

MAKING IT LAST
Dancing is hard, sweaty work, so we always choose makeup products that are waterproof, made for all-day wear, and/or semipermanent. Some products easily replace others; for example, waterproof colored mascara

makes great eyeshadow and liner. Use a cotton swab to apply it, so you don't damage your brushes (or just use old brushes), and your makeup will stay put all night. Similarly, semipermanent lipstick also makes a terrific blush that won't slide down your face when it gets hot and you start to sweat. Just make sure you blend it in quickly and thoroughly after you apply.

GLAMA PAM

Here are the in-depth directions to using stripper makeup. This is an intense look, so if you are not a stripper, do this only if you are going out clubbing or on a music-video shoot. If you'd like to try this for a daytime look, just use lighter colors like beige and taupe instead of black and brown. Oh, and blend really, really well.

To begin: Start with foundation if you need it. Apply concealer under your eyes, over both entire eyelids, and over any zits you might have. Blend. Line your upper eyelids just above the lash line with black liquid waterproof liner. You can substitute dark brown or gray liner if you have very fair skin or are afraid of looking too harsh. Wait a minute or two for the liner to dry, then dust it with loose powder to set it. If you use it, apply lip builder (as directed above) and dust it with powder to set it. If not, just apply your regular lip liner and dust it with powder.

Moving back up to the eyes, take a large shadow brush and apply a shimmery white shadow over the entire lid, using a little more on the brow bone for a stronger shimmer. Next, take a small shadow brush and apply a black, dark brown, or dark gray shadow in the crease of your eyelid, sweeping the color gently outward. You want the shadow in the crease to look really intense, so make sure you apply enough to get this effect. Using a cotton swab or a precision shadow brush, apply the same crease color along your lower eyelid from corner to corner, following and staying as close as possible to your lash line. If you have large eyes or want to rock an even more intense look, line the rim of your lower eyelid with the dark shadow as well. Yes, you will end up with some powder in your eyes, but relax! It only hurts for a second.

Next, take a large makeup brush, dip it in loose powder, and dust over your eyeshadow until the colors are well blended. If the crease color becomes too light, just apply more. Going back to the lips, line them over the lip builder just outside your natural lip line in a deep nude shade. The color shouldn't be so dark that it looks like eyeliner, or so light that you can't see it. Using a clean finger, blend the lip-liner color downward onto your lip. Apply a frosty pink or peach lipstick (whichever best suits your skin tone) and a coat of thick lip gloss. Okay. Your lips and eyes are done. For the final touch, take a separate large powder brush, dip it into bronzing powder, blow off any excess, and apply to cheeks, chin, nose, and temples. Apply a bit to your neck too, so there isn't a tonal difference and your makeup doesn't look like a mask. Dust your entire face with loose powder to set everything. Finally, apply a set of false eyelashes in black or dark brown, using the directions given at the beginning of this section. Voilà! You have mastered the Pam.

PART II: THE SAVAGE TAN

Strippers are usually tanned to golden perfection, some spending several hours a week at tanning salons. For those who don't want to spend their retirement money on biopsies and chemotherapy, faking it is the best way to glow.

Self-Tanners

A self-tanner works by reacting to the melanin level in your skin. The darker your skin, the darker your tan will be. Tanners generally come in three shades: light, medium, and dark. If you have very pale skin or burn easily when you go out in the sun, choose a light color for the most natural look.

TANNER SELECTION

Tanners come in creams, gels, and sprays. Some creams and gels have a bronze tint to them. Aside from giving you a little color immediately, these also allow you to see if you missed a spot in one area or need to blend it in another. The color tends to be quite sparkly, which looks great at night or out at a club but way too harsh and fake in the light of day. Personally, I prefer the sprays because they dry the fastest. Having tried virtually every brand of tanner, I can say that the stuff they sell at drugstores is pretty much the same as the stuff they sell at cosmetics counters. Every product works differently on everybody, so you might find that a pricier brand works better on you than a drugstore brand. If that's the case, stick with what you like. Just keep in mind that a designer product will not necessarily buy you a better-looking tan. My favorite tanner brands are Bain de Soleil (Radiance Eternelle only), Giesee (by Sun Labratories), and St. Tropez. These three are tinted, so they give you an immediate glow, but they're not shimmery, so you can apply them and go. They also get my skin the darkest, which is, of course, the primary goal. If you do want to sparkle, I like Lancôme's Flash Bronzer for legs. It has a rich, bright shimmer and a pleasant scent. It's the perfect choice if you're going out and you want to highlight and deepen your existing tan. The actual tanner in it won't get you dark, however, so choose something else if that's what you're looking for.

For the record, my least favorite brand is Neutrogena, which has a tendency to turn orange and will not—despite the label's promise—get you "extra-deep." Estée Lauder is also awful. The color is too orange, and it has the unfortunate tendency to shed off in weird, molting snake–like flakes. Not an attractive look on, or wearing off. Unfortunately, finding the right product for you will take some trial and error. The tips below should help.

TO APPLY

First, it's important to exfoliate well before each self-tanner application. Next, you want to put a light coat of moisturizer over any rough or dry skin patches you have, such as on your ankles, knees, elbows, or armpits.

I find the best way to apply tanner is to wear a pair of thin cotton manicure gloves over a pair of plastic or latex gloves. The plastic layer will protect your fingers and nails from getting stained, and the cotton will help you rub in the tanner. Don't forget your neck, ears, tops of hands, feet, and armpits. Have someone help you get your back, or do this instead: Spray the tanner or place the gel or cream as close to the area you're unable to reach as possible. Next, take an old towel between both hands and gently pull it across your back a few times. This will distribute the tanner evenly onto the uncovered area. It will probably still be a little paler than the rest of your fake tan, but it shouldn't be noticeable. Although it's important to evenly distribute the tanner, don't rub too much. Overrubbing can actually remove tanner from your skin, resulting in uneven patches or streaks. Stroke it on, but remember that allowing your skin to *absorb* the tanner will result in better coverage. Even if you are using a spray or other fast-drying formula, try to stay naked or in a loose-fitting robe for at least an hour after the application. This will prevent the color from rubbing off on your clothes and the tan from developing unevenly on you.

Most tanners claim that the color will develop in one or two hours. In reality, it usually takes between five and six hours for the color to reach its full intensity. To get the most color out of a self-tanner application, wait a full twenty-four hours after an application before showering. Your color will be richer.

While a fake bake is the safest choice, a major drawback to self-tanner is that you have to live with your mistakes until the color fades. If this happens, two good at-home exfoliants are: a mixture of lemon juice and sea salt for oily skin; or course sugar and uncooked rice mixed with water or a skin-friendly oil, such as almond or jojoba, for dry skin. Your run-of-the-mill apricot-type scrub or loofah pad will work well too. After you exfoliate, apply an alpha-hydroxy-based moisturizer to turn over your dead skin cells faster. (Obviously, don't try *any* of these suggestions if you have sensitive skin or any kind of cut or abrasion.)

Still, in my opinion, the worst problem with self-tanner is that it smells. The odor is hard to describe, but it's something like damp old socks. The stink is the strongest after you apply it, but you can still smell it a couple of days later, especially when you sweat. If you're a dancer, this usually isn't a problem because men are focused on other things, like the naked boobs in front of them. However, it's always wise to carry around a bottle of lightly scented body spray in case you start to feel self-conscious.

Mist Beds

Some tanning salons, in addition to tanning beds, offer booths that spray self-tanner on for you. You change into a bathing suit (or go naked, if you want an all-over glow) and step into what looks like an ordinary tanning booth. But instead of the UV lights coming on, a fine mist of self-tanner comes out, giving you a quick, even coat. You step in and—*bam!*—five minutes later, you're tan.

While there's no faster, easier way to apply self-tanner, one major drawback is the price: Mist beds start at around twenty-five dollars a squirt. This is fine if you're using tanner for a one-time event, like a cocktail party that your ex will be attending, but if you are committed to looking tan for the long haul, you'll need to go at least twice a week to keep up the glow. At a minimum, you're spending two hundred dollars a month, when one bottle of good tanner is about twenty dollars and will last at least that long. Another problem with mist beds is that at some places you still have to rub it in, which, unless you're using rubber gloves, still means the risk of orange palms. And no matter how great the technology, you still can't get away from that smell.

Airbrush Tan

Another new self-tanning technology developed on the West Coast has recently arrived in the East. For about eighty-five dollars a pop, a technician will hose you down with tinted self-tanner from an airbrush. You can get an even color all over or have her use different-colored tanners to sculpt you some abs. While those who have tried it say this application method is tops, it's still *eighty-five dollars.* And since if you're careful you can get the same exact results at home, unless you're especially rich or especially lazy, the process is just not worth it.

Combination Tans

If you are absolutely desperate for a quick glow, one easy way is to hit a low-intensity tanning bed for twenty minutes. Use a low-SPF sunscreen (unless you are going to a state-of-the-art tanning salon, like Portofino). Otherwise, all those little coffin-beds *burn.* When you're done, shower if you've applied sunscreen, and then apply self-tanner. The tanner will react with the newly produced melanin in your skin, leaving you looking like you just got back from spring break. Whatever you do, do *not* apply the tanner *before* hitting the tanning bed, because your sweat will cause the color to develop unevenly. Also, it's important to wait about an hour after tanning to take a shower—the tanning session will cause you to sweat, which will continue for a little while after it's over.

Obviously, this is not good for your skin, but it is an easy way to make sure jaws drop. A final word about self-tanners: They tend to dry out your skin, so use a nice moisturizing soap or, better yet, a soap-free body wash when you exfoliate. On days when you are not applying tanner, slather yourself in a rich moisturizer after you shower.

STRIPPER TIPS!

BUST ON OUT

If you are a natural girl or are self-conscious about size, the best way to make your boobs stand out is to frame them with tan lines. Guys, for whatever reason, love tan lines. You don't actually need a tan; you can use self-tanner or bronzer to mimic the lines of a bikini bra top. You can do this by hand, or you can just apply tanner or makeup over an old bathing suit. Be careful, because self-tanner will stain any clothing it touches. Wait until your tan develops, then highlight the pale part of your breast with a gold or silver body shimmer. The contrast between your pale breasts and tan skin will make your breasts look larger.

Sometimes having very large nipples can make your boobs look small. To change your nipple size, apply a very light or white concealer over the outside of the areola (as much of it as you want to hide), then pat over with a concealer that matches the color of the skin on your breast. Your best bet is to use an industrial-strength concealer like Dermablend, made especially for hard-to-hide problems like birthmarks or scars. Set the concealer with loose powder. You can also see your dermatologist about fruit-acid peels or lightening cream to reduce some of the pigmentation that comes with childbirth or topless sunbathing.

EIGHT-SECOND ABS

If you are feeling particularly bloated or flabby, this is a great trick to give you instant abs. Apply self-tanner all over, as you normally would. Then suck in your stomach. Next, apply a little extra or slightly darker shade of self-tanner up and down along the outside of your oblique muscles. When the color develops, your stomach will have the same contours as a naturally ripped tum!

If you want to get the look of a six-pack, first define your obliques, then draw on three horizontal lines just below each muscle. (Again, suck in your stomach to locate them.)

THE THIGH-MASTER

Again, after you've applied your normal shade of self-tanner, apply either a little extra or a slightly darker shade to your butt, thighs, and/or saddlebags. The eye will be drawn away from your darker lower body and toward your lighter upper body, helping to visually balance out your proportions.

If you have naturally dark skin or don't want to use self-tanner but need a little boost, temporary tanning products are great. These are:

Bronzer

The most popular product with dancers is bronzing powder. We use it all over our bodies, after we've hit the salon or the self-tanner has dried. These come in a variety of shades and are available at almost any cosmetics counter. Bronzers are easy to apply (just a brush!), don't smell, and leave your skin looking silky tan. You can dust it on your legs, chest, neck, and face for a quick golden glow. The main drawback of using a bronzing powder is that it will rub off on your clothes, so make sure you wear dark colors if you are using it all over.

STRIPPER TIPS!

You can use bronzing powder in addition to, or instead of, self-tanner to get eight-second abs or a smaller-looking butt. If you're going out and want to wear something low-cut and sexy, you can also maximize your cleavage with bronzer. Start with a large powder brush. Dip it into the bronzer and sweep it between your breasts, then up and over the top of each breast in an arc. Apply more bronzer than you think is necessary, to get a good contrast between the skin color on your breasts and the skin color between them. Next, blow off the excess bronzer on your brush and blend the bronzer from your chest onto your breasts, so the color has a natural look to it. The contrast between your tan chest and paler breasts will make them look fuller and rounder.

Gel

A great stripper secret is Clinque's Skin Supplies for Men Non-Streak Bronzer. Just one or two applications of this lightweight gel and you have a really dark, natural-looking tan. It smells great, dries instantly, and has minimum rub-off. Plus, it's not shimmery, so it looks like skin, not makeup. The application will stain your hands a little bit, and you have to rub it in quickly to avoid having it dry in streaks. Most dancers mix it with a little moisturizer to help it blend. In my experience, the worst problem with this product is that it's water-soluble. The manufacturer says that it comes off with *soap* and water, but that's not true. Just a little bit of water will do. So don't wear it to the water park, or on really hot days when you could sweat it off. This also means that you need to take care if you sweat a lot or in certain places (under your breasts, for instance).

Aerosol

My absolute favorite product is called Aerotan, made by Sex Symbol. Basically, it's tan in a can. You spray it on, and your skin instantly takes on a deep, shimmery golden tan. It smells like a piña colada and leaves your skin feeling smooth. There is minimal rub-off, so it won't look blotchy or turn your clothes orange. And because it washes off with soap and water, your hands won't give you away. Since the color is pretty dark, you'll need to have someone get your back. A FINAL NOTE: Aerotan is an aerosol, so make sure you spray it only in a *really* well-ventilated room.

Tinted Moisturizer

Every cosmetics company makes a shimmery moisturizer for face and body. Dancers like BeneFit's Flamingo Fancy, which is a dark pinkish gold. Tinted moisturizers are great if your skin is naturally dark or if you're using it over self-tanner. Light gold or silver shimmers like those found in BeneFit's Lightning body lotion are best for highlighting and drawing attention to certain areas, like your cleavage. They also help smooth out your skin tone. However, stay away from the shimmer if you're breaking out—it will just draw attention to your zits. Lovely, eh?

Baby Oil

The most effective quick fix for blah winter skin is baby oil. Every strip club has a bottle in the dressing room. It makes your skin appear darker and leaves it feeling buttery smooth. Most dancers prefer Johnson's Baby Oil in gel formula. It's easier to apply, since you're not holding a handful of oil, and feels less greasy. Plus, the gel formulas have a more grown-up scent, so you won't walk around smelling like diapers. Baby oil is not shimmery and won't dye your skin, which is a big plus if you're just looking for a subtle boost.

STRIPPER TIPS!

As you've noticed, looking tan year-round has hit the mainstream—virtually every major line of department-store cosmetics offers self-tanning products, bronzers, and oils to make your skin look darker. If you like to use these products but don't want to spend a lot, here are some easy ways to get these same looks on the cheap:

TINTED MOISTURIZER
Go to you local drugstore's cosmetics section and find the cheapest loose bronzing powder you can. Some terrific low-price labels include Wet 'n' Wild, Jane, and CornSilk. Next, mix the powder into the moisturizer you are

already using. Check the color as you mix by rubbing it on the back of your hand. Use just a little powder if you want a slight tint, a lot if you want to go really dark.

BODY OILS

Instead of buying pricey "dry oils" (basically a blend of fast-absorbing, nongreasy oils), you can make your own body spray by going to a health-food store and buying a skin-friendly oil like almond or jojoba and pouring it into a spray bottle. Of course, the easiest route is to use plain suntan oil. Many companies, such as Banana Boat, make low-SPF suntan oils that come in handy spray bottles. Most of them already have that great beachy smell, and the bottles are refillable. You can also add shimmer if you want; just follow the steps for making the moisturizer above, adding a little bronzer at a time until you get the desired shade. Do be careful, because spray bottles have a tendency to clog, so make sure you use loose powder, and keep a light touch. With oil, less is always more.

OTHER TIPS

- Instead of bronzing powder, you can add a loose, shimmery white (not silver—you will look undead) or gold eye shadow to the moisturizer or oil.
- You can also funk it up a little by adding iridescent powdered eyeshadow in an unusual color, like magenta, turquoise, or coral.

PART III: HAIR

Okay, I'm just going to say it: Men love long hair. They may like
short hair on their wives, girlfriends, or mothers, but when it
comes to topless dancers, the hands-down preference is for long,
sexy locks. Long hair is usually the only difference between looking cute and looking hot. When I first started dancing I had short,
blond Meg Ryan hair. I made money, but certainly not the kind of
money I had hoped for. A friend of mine (a seasoned pro with ten
years of dancing under her garter) recommended I get hair extensions. I took her advice and an amazing thing happened: My
money skyrocketed!

Length

Whether you want to increase your length a little or a lot, and you
don't want to wait, the best thing to do is to get hair extensions.
With hair extensions, real human hair is attached to your own.
Salons use a couple of different techniques; bonding and weaving.
There is a new technology coming out that involves using Scotch
tape (?!) but as of this writing, it's still in the experimental stage.

BONDING

The best and most natural-looking kind of extensions is bonding,
also called glue extensions. With the right cut, these extensions
blend perfectly, and they are the easiest to wash and style (just
like your own hair). Sarah Michelle Gellar, Jennifer Lopez, and
Christina Aguilera have all sported this type of hair extension.

Unfortunately, the process itself is long, painful, and pricey.
First the weaver takes tiny bundles of human hair and vertically

braids them in with your own hair. The small braid is then set with glue and heated with an iron to bond it. (Don't worry: The glue will not damage your hair.) This is repeated wherever necessary to achieve the length or layers you want. For a full head of hair, be prepared to spend 6–10 hours in the salon and around a thousand dollars for the process. Just adding a little length to the back will obviously take less time and be less expensive. You can also have just a few extensions put in here and there if you like the look of highlights but don't want to damage your natural hair. Prices vary from salon to salon, so call around first to get the best price.

WEAVING

Black hair salons pioneered the classic hair-weave technique. The process involves making thin, tight cornrows of your own hair in horizontal "tracks" along your scalp. The weaver then sews wefts (human hair that has been attached onto a thread of sorts) into the cornrows. If the tracks are placed well and blended into your own hairline, weaves can look completely natural. Weaves are cheaper and take a little less time than bonding, but they are every bit as painful. The tight cornrows and the weight of the tracks on them will cause your scalp to hurt for a few days, until your hair grows a bit and lessens up the tension. It isn't possible, however, to have the weaver make the cornrows less tight—the tracks won't sit right on your head if she does. The cool thing about weaving is that you don't need to go to a salon to do it. You can pick up the wefts at many beauty-supply stores, and if you have a friend who knows how to cornrow, she can do it for you. Sewing in the wefts is the easy (if time-consuming) part. I actually worked with a girl who did her own weaves. She would cornrow her own hair, then sew her wefts in while she was sitting around reading the paper or watching TV. I don't recommend trying this at home if you're a hair-weave beginner, but if you have some experience and some time, it might be fun.

CLIP-ONS

The cheapest, easiest way to get a little length is to buy a hair-piece. It's a great party look, popularized by the character Carrie on HBO's *Sex and the City.* These come in lots of styles, so you can do a long Tomb Raider–style ponytail, sassy braids, or even a sophisticated upsweep. Most of the larger drugstore chains now carry clip-ons, and virtually all beauty-supply stores carry them as well. Choose a color that matches your own, clip on, and go.

STRIPPER TIPS!

Most clip-on hairpieces and falls are made out of synthetic (i.e., nonhuman) hair. Synthetic hair is really healthy- and shiny-looking; and herein lies the problem. It's too healthy and shiny—which is the dead giveaway that it's not your own. If it's a wig it'll look too "perfect," and if it's a fall or clip-on, the texture of the hair won't match. One way strippers "rough up" the look of a synthetic piece is by adding baby powder or hair powder (colored powdered shampoo) to dull down the shine a bit. However, don't go overboard using styling products on synthetic hair—it comes prestyled. Hairspray, gels, and mousses won't reshape a style you don't like. In addition, too much hairspray can cause the strands to lump together in an unflattering and unnatural way. It's best to

use just a light dusting of spray, and only if you think
you need it.

WARNING: *Do not use heated styling tools on synthetic
hair!* This includes hair dryers, curling irons,
straightening irons, and heated curlers. Any of these tools
will cause synthetic hair to melt or, worse, catch on fire.

Hair Color

Strip clubs are dark. Really, really dark. This is for two reasons: 1)
The girls always look hot, and 2) You can never see their cellulite—even when a girl's butt is only inches away from your face.
Because clubs are so dark, most girls go with extreme hair colors
to help them stand out. Blondes are platinum, reds are electric,
and brunettes are glossy coffee brown or blue-black. Girls who go
with highlights generally favor big chunky blond streaks around
their hairline and crown, fading to a darker blond or even light
brown underneath and toward the back. *Subtle* and *well blended*
are not the usual adjectives used to describe stripper hair. Think
more of big, bold Hollywood glamour hair and you get the picture.

Your best bet is to gather pictures of a celebrity whose hair color
you like and bring them with you to a salon. It's expensive, yes, but
hair color is so important that it's worth thinking of it as an invest-
ment. Save the money you would spend doing it yourself at home—
and the additional amount you would fork over trying to correct
your mistakes—and get it done right the first time. This isn't to say
that you need to spend a lot of money; in fact, I recommend that
you don't. While you're not going to get high-quality color at
Supercuts, many higher-end salons offer "student nights" where

they train up-and-coming stylists and colorists. You can get a cut or color for free or pay a very small fraction of the salon's usual price. Another option is to do a hair show. Lots of cities across the country participate in hair shows, where, as in fashion shows, models wear the latest colors and cuts. However, unlike fashion shows, the models aren't anorexic twigs—in fact, they're just everyday men and women. Most hair salons will advertise before a show, saying something like "hair models needed." They're a lot of fun; plus, you get to have your hair done by a professional for free.

That said, if you're determined to do it yourself, here are some tips:

- If you have virgin hair, meaning that it's never been colored before, you can use over-the-counter products to change your color. I like L'Oréal Feria because they give you an extra-big bottle of color so you don't have to worry about running out if you have longer hair. You can generally go lighter or darker, within one to two shades of your natural color, without incurring much damage. You can also add a new tone, so if you have light brown hair, for example, and you want to add some red tones, a light auburn shade will work for you.

- You can cover any gray hairs you have by dyeing your hair the same color as your original hair. You can also cover gray by choosing a lighter color than your hair and using a *nonammonia* formula such as L'Oréal ColorSpa or Clairol's Loving Care.

- You can do your own highlights. Most companies offer their own highlighting kits, such as L'Oréal Couleur Experte or Clairol Herbal Essences Highlights. These kits use a small plastic "brush" that you dip into the dye and streak through your hair. Although this technique is less time-consuming than the classic cap-and-hook method, you also have a lot less control. And control is crucial when it comes to creating natural-looking highlights. For this reason, I recommend using a brand like Clairol Frost & Tip, which offers the cap and hook. It is time-consuming to pull all your hair through (and can be kind of painful), but the results will be worth it.

- If, after having done your highlights, you find that you have gone too light, that they don't blend well with your natural color, or that they have a weird tone to them, such as yellow or orange, you can use a toner. To tone your highlights yourself, pick up a box of a nonammonia haircolor like Clairol Loving Care or L'Oréal ColorSpa. If your hair's too light or your highlights aren't blending in well, pick a color two or three shades lighter than your natural color. If your highlights turned out yellow, choose a light shade with a beige or "violet" base. If your highlights look red or orange, choose an ash shade. Follow the directions on the box, and your highlights should come out looking fantastic.

Strip Club Styles

Some strip clubs have rules about how you can wear your hair. For example, some allow dancers to wear hairpieces, ponytails, braids, or upsweeps, and some require dancers to wear their hair down. The club where I work allows dancers to wear hairpieces and all varieties of hairstyles, which is nice, because even with all the time and effort dancers put into styling their hair, sometimes it refuses to submit, no matter how much pressure—or product—we put on it. For us, as for you, it's always good to have options. For girls who do choose to wear their hair up, the top three styles are the ponytail, braids, and the upsweep.

DO THE PONY

It's really unlikely that anyone reading this needs tips on how to put her hair into a ponytail. If you are like most women, chances are you frequently wear your hair in a ponytail. However, there are a few things you should know about how strippers do their ponies. Long hair looks best if it is sleeked back away from your face and gathered in back, toward the middle of your head. Think Lara Croft without the braid. It's simple, pretty, and will draw attention to your face and tan. Longer medium-length hair also looks good in this style, but you may want to use a straightening iron and some antifrizz serum to make sure that the actual ponytail doesn't get too poufy. Shorter medium-length hair and short hair look best with a low, nape-of-neck ponytail. In this case, you may need to use antifrizz serum and/or a firm-holding hairspray on the top of your head to keep any shorter pieces from coming undone. You can also use bobby pins that match your hair color to keep shorter underneath hairs in place.

PIGTAILS

Only girls under the age of nine and strippers over the age of twenty-one sport this style. It's frankly indecent for anyone else. Still, it's definitely worth trying them out on your man in the privacy of the bedroom, because they are a tried-and-true method of driving him crazy. Pigtails work on any length hair (except, of course, boy-cut short). Go for high pigtails by taking a comb and forming a part right down the middle of your head. Gather the hair on either side into a pigtail on the high side of the crown of your head, and secure with an elastic band. Make sure that the hair flowing into each pigtail is smoothly gathered (for this reason it sometimes helps to use a brush or comb to do the gathering). It looks okay, though, if some shorter hairs at the nape of your neck hang down, or if you leave some fringe around your face. Higher pigtails are younger- and naughtier-looking; wear them only if you or your partner is dying to try out the sexy-schoolgirl fantasy. Low pigtails, on the other hand, are a more mature look. They have that wholesome farmer's daughter, country girl, or college cheerleader appeal. To get low pigtails, again, use a comb to part your hair down the middle. Make sure the hair is smooth as you form each pigtail and secure each side with a simple hair elastic. You can spice up either high or low pigtails with accessorized hairbands—choose ones with electric colors, big bright beads, or even little feather poufs to make it more interesting. With low pigtails, it's important that you do have some bangs or fringe left out to frame your face—otherwise you can look a little Wednesday Addams or American Gothic (especially with dark hair).

BRAIDS

A Tomb Raider–style long braid is a great alternative to a ponytail. It's sleek and polished-looking but also a little exotic. It looks especially sexy if you pair it with a deep tan and some red lipstick. For this, all you need to do is sleek your hair back into a ponytail with a hair elastic. It's actually best to do this when your hair is dripping wet from the shower; you'll get a stronger, sleeker line. Next, just braid the length of your hair and secure the end with another elastic. Smooth some antifrizz serum into the length of the braid to prevent any ends from flying out, or use extra-strength gel if your hair is especially unruly.

A stripper favorite is the look of two low Indian-maiden braids. It's a supersexy style that's more grown-up than low pigtails and more exotic than a plain pony. For this, just follow the steps above to make two low pigtails. Then braid each pigtail and secure with another hair elastic. You'll also need some antifrizz stuff or hair gel, especially if you have shorter hair or layers, because with these cuts, braids will have a tendency to look bulky.

FRENCH BRAIDS

Most dancers stay away from French-braiding their hair for a very good reason: Wearing your hair in French braids is code that you're into S&M. It lets customers know that you're either *dominant,* meaning someone who enjoys spanking grown men in face masks and rubber diapers, or that you are submissive, meaning someone who might like to be spanked while wearing a face mask and rubber diapers. If this is something you enjoy, then by all means, braid it up. For the most part, though, strip clubs don't attract this kind of dancer or audience. And while it's rare that we get customers who are into that sort of thing, it happens often enough that unless you really are looking for a slave, you don't want to accidentally advertise for one.

THE UPSWEEP

Clean, classy-looking upsweeps, the kind you see in fine jewelry ads and *Dynasty* reruns, take a lot of effort to do, a lot of pins to keep up, and a lot of hairspray to hold in place. Luckily, strippers tend to avoid anything that falls into the "classy" category—especially when it comes to hair. The stripper upsweep is sexy and messy. There are a few ways you can do it, depending on how much time you have and what tools are at your disposal. The most complicated upsweep involves hairpins, so if you're going to try it, make sure you have some that blend in with your hair color. Working with hairpins can be tricky; give yourself a few practice runs so you're not totally stressed trying to do your hair before a big event. This particular upsweep also looks best on hair that is shoulder length or longer.

First, brush out your hair so it's tangle-free and smooth. If your hair is baby-fine or really healthy, it will help if you put in some texturizing cream or gel, such as Sheer Blonde Funky Chunky. It'll give your hair some weight and form so that it won't keep slipping out of style. Once your hair is brushed and the product in, gather it in a low ponytail, slightly above the nape of your neck. (Again, make sure you leave a little hair loose up front to frame your face.) You'll want to start gathering the hair for the ponytail about an inch behind your hairline. This way, the hair around your face can be curled or styled to create a sexy frame. Next, begin twisting the base of the ponytail and attach it to your head with hairpins as you go up. You'll know you have the hairpin in securely if it hurts like a beotch. Keep twisting and pinning the hair until you have just rounded the crown of your head. Arrange the hair that is left evenly to either side of the upsweep, so that you have sexy, messy tendrils hanging down. You might need to use a wide (one-inch diameter or more) curling iron to give the ends of your hair, and the hair you left out around your face, some bend and shape. (If you find that you've left too much hair out up front, you can easily brush it back and pin it into the twist.) Finally, take an extra-firm-hold hairspray and spray the living daylights out of the back where you have twisted it. You should have a sexy do that will last, no matter how many times your dress comes on or off.

Pinning your hair does look great, but even this messy style can look overdone if you are just running around in jeans and a tee. Your best bet for an even more casual upsweep is to try a double-backed ponytail. This style works best on short, shorter medium-length, and layered hair. First, brush out your hair and apply a texturizing product as necessary. Next, pull your hair back into a high ponytail—it should rest at the very back part of the top of your head—and secure it with an elastic. (Again, start the ponytail about an inch back from your hairline, so you can create a fringe.) Next, take your ponytail and tuck it about halfway back through the elastic. This should create a cute little pouf on top of your head. Pull some strands completely free, and tuck some under as necessary to create a pretty look.

The easiest way to do an upsweep is to leave a front fringe and gather the rest of your hair in a low ponytail, then begin twisting it up, like you would if you were going to pin it. Instead of using hairpins to secure it, simply use a butterfly clip. Choose one that is long enough and wide enough to accommodate all your hair (extra-thick or long hair might need the additional support of a few bobby pins to hold it in). Placing the clip low will create a clean, classic look, while a higher-placed clip will give you some height and some sexy stray tendrils to play with.

For Curly Girls

The 1980s and early '90s were halcyon days for curly-haired girls. Attitudes were big, shoulder pads were big, and hair was the biggest of all. If you think back to all the blockbuster movies of this period, you realize that every female lead had a full head of lush curls streaming down her back. Jennifer Beals in *Flashdance:* curly. Kim Basinger in *9 ½ Weeks:* curly. Darryl Hannah in *Splash:* curly. Debra Winger in *Terms of Endearment:* again, curly. Even Meg Ryan had long, curly hair in the classic *When Harry Met Sally.* Of course, it was really Julia Roberts in her breakout performance in *Pretty Woman* that brought curly hair into vogue. In high school, it seemed like everyone and her mom rushed out to the local beauty salon to throw a perm in. My friends and I all got one—even though I already had curly hair. Sadly, for those of us blessed (or cursed) with it, having curly hair has been out of style for a good long while. Here are some of the ways we manage:

THERMAL RESTRUCTURING

At strip clubs, most girls with naturally curly hair choose to get their hair straightened professionally by a process developed in Japan called "thermal restructuring." This is basically a healthier version of the old heat-and-lye relaxer that black women and women with very curly hair have been using for decades. While thermal restructuring does seem to work well and, better yet, can be used on color-treated hair, the process is expensive (about eighty-five dollars every four to six weeks). Another drawback is that you'll get roots while your hair is growing out. This means that you'll still have to use a straightening iron to avoid having a weird-looking curly root/straight hair contrast.

BLOWOUTS

Many chain salons, like Supercuts, Jean Louis David, and Dramatics, will wash and blow-dry your hair for you, for about twenty dollars a pop. While this might sound indulgent to some (what, you can't wash your hair by yourself?), it's actually a really good option for curly-haired women committed to the straight-hair lifestyle. First, curly hair tends to by dry, so most hair-care experts recommend washing it only once or twice a week anyway. Second, it's hard to give yourself a good blowout without damaging your hair. So if you have the extra cash, you can save yourself some time and aggravation by having a professional do it for you. Plus, you'll know that no matter what, your hair always looks fantastic.

STRAIGHTENING IRONS

The most effective way to straighten your hair at home is by using a straightening iron. These are sold at most drugstores, where they keep their hair-care products and blow-dryers. Any drugstore brand will work well if you have an average amount of hair with a slight wave to it. If you have very thick, wavy, or curly hair, you'll need to go to a beauty-supply shop and get a professional straightener; drugstore brands will not get hot enough to get your hair bone-straight. My personal favorite is the 160-watt straightener by BaByliss. It heats up quickly and gets my hair superflat in no time. If you will be straightening your hair at home, you'll want to wash your hair only a couple of times a week anyway; all heated styling tools will damage your hair to some degree—there'll be more damage the more often you use them.

CERAMICS

The new technology in straightening and curling irons is ceramic.

Before, they were always made of metal. Many hairstylists prefer ceramic irons because they conduct heat better than the metal, and thus they work more quickly, using less heat. Because they use less heat, ceramic irons tend to be less damaging to your hair. The major drawback to ceramics is that they are way more expensive than similar metal ones—a good ceramic straightener can cost as much as two hundred dollars.

Au Naturel

Some dancers refuse to let their looks be dictated by popular style and let their curls hang out in all their glory. If you want to, these three tools are a must:

1. A good antifrizz serum. My personal favorite is BioSilk. It's lightweight and nongreasy, which is key, especially if you have oily hair.
2. A curling iron with a diameter that matches your natural curl. Even if you have tight ringlets, you'll need a curling iron to blend in any and all stray hairs that refuse to submit.
3. A hairdryer with a diffuser. While we know that you won't catch a cold if you leave the house with wet hair, you'll still feel cold. A diffuser will dry your hair without blowing out the curl.

Other recommended products for curly hair:

Frizz-Ease antifrizz serum by John Frieda. This is a thicker formula that works well on dry and especially unruly hair.
Beach Blonde Ocean Waves, also by John Frieda. This

combination of sea salt and conditioning oils brings tired curls back to life. It also has the nicest, beachiest scent, which is a great perk-up in the dead of winter.

PART IV: NAILS

Manicures

Long, manicured, well-kept nails indicate a well-kept woman. And men love women who take care of themselves. For those of you used to a life of leisure, having long nails and finding the time to maintain them isn't a problem. For those of you who live in the real world and must work at real jobs, long nails can seem like more trouble than they're worth. However, the truth is that nails don't need to be really long to look sexy. Short, polished, well-groomed nails will sex up any look and make even the most casual outfit look hotter.

THE BASIC

For healthy nails, natural is better. It's easier, cheaper, and better for your nails if you just grow them out yourself, and go to a nail salon once a week for a massage and a fresh coat of paint. There are a lot of other reasons why natural nails are better, but they are best learned from the examples below.

SILK WRAPS

The silk wrap involves gluing a piece of silk fabric to your natural nails to make them stronger and keep them from breaking. These are useful if you have very thin, brittle nails or have the kind of job (landscaper, chef, housekeeper) that puts a lot of stress on your nails. After the silk is glued into place, you just get a regular manicure. The wraps last a couple of weeks; you may need to go in every other week for maintenance if a wrap comes unglued.

SILK EXTENSIONS

Silk extensions are basically silk wraps that add length. Instead of cutting the piece of silk where your nail ends, the manicurist extends it outward. Using a combination of glue, powder, more glue, and a small electric sander (I'm not kidding), she forms a solid, hard-as-steel fake nail, which she then trims and buffs and manicures like a normal nail. This process is generally the most expensive of the different types of manicures, generally takes the longest, and is thought of as the healthiest form of fake nail you can apply.

ACRYLICS

As of this writing, acrylic tips are illegal in New York City because the acrylic sealer poses a health risk. You can buy acrylic-nail kits at larger drugstores, so if they're not available at a salon near you, you can apply them yourself. Either way, be prepared to spend a good two hours for the application process. You will also need to reapply glue, powder, and acrylic once a week to keep the nail attached. Once every two or three weeks you'll need another set put on, which means starting the process all over again.

PRESS-ON NAILS

These are good in theory, bad in reality. The nails come in

assorted sizes and/or colors, and stick to your nail (usually) with a small piece of strong, double-sided adhesive. Press-ons are probably the best solution to the broken-nail-ten-minutes-before-the-cocktail-party dilemma, when your range of movement will be limited to lifting a champagne flute to your mouth. Anything more strenuous than this—say, repeatedly tucking twenty-dollar bills into your garter—will cause the nail to unglue. You'll spend the rest of the night either obsessively pressing your nails down to make sure the glue sticks or searching for your lost nails on the floor.

NOTE: Upkeep of silk wraps, extensions, and acrylics is important, because moisture can get between your real nail and the nail tip. If this happens, your fingernail will become a virtual petri dish for all sorts of bacteria and infections. Finally, fake nails are time-consuming and expensive. Nice-looking nails are important, but it is up to you how much they're worth.

COLOR

The classic stripper nail is the French manicure with either a buff- or pink-toned nail bed and a bright white tip. I associate the French manicure so strongly with dancers and celebrities like Pamela Anderson and Britney Spears that I feel a little naughty sporting them in the light of day. However, the colors are neutral enough to wear with any outfit, and they look great on short nails, as well as longer ones.

Other stripper favorites are a superfrosty white and baby pink. My mood for color changes with the seasons, so I tend to wear lighter colors and pastels in the spring and stronger variations of these in the summer. In the fall and winter I might go with a deep fuchsia, but I avoid fiery reds and really dark Goth colors like Chanel's Vamp because they can look a little too dragon-lady in the club.

Pedicures

Dancers always make sure their feet are nicely pedicured. At some clubs, women wear open-toed heels, so nice toes are necessary. At my club, we wear only closed-toe stilettos, so guys never actually ever see our feet. Still, you never know when some freak with a fetish will offer you a thousand dollars just to see your toes (it does happen), so it's always wise to be prepared. Besides, nothing's less sexy than scraggly toe talons growing in every direction.

For color, the hottest look is the French pedicure. It uses the same colors and procedure as the French manicure, and it looks every bit as sexy on your feet as it does on your hands. However, there is no need for your fingernails and toenails to match. And if you want to go wild, your toes are a great place to start. Funk it up with a not-appropriate-for-the-office color like bright blue, yellow, or shocking pink.

PART V: GROOMING

The Hair Down There

Men strongly prefer that their ladies be well groomed—everywhere. I know it's not fair; men (usually) don't do it, so why should we? Although I could wax philosophical about this, as a stripper I have no choice. When your work uniform is a G-string, pubic hair is an accessory you can't afford to have. There are several methods of hair removal on the market—what will work for you depends mostly on how much time you can devote each week to elimination of unwanted hair and how high your pain threshold is.

WAXING

For a cost of between fifteen and fifty dollars, a salon will apply hot wax to your skin and rip out all your pubic hair. It's painful, yes, but it's still the preferred method. Waxing leaves your skin smooth and hair-free for up to three weeks. Plus, there are lots of styles to choose from: the landing strip, the heart shape, the Brazilian. Get a new one every month! All kidding aside, waxing isn't for everyone. Skip it if you have really sensitive skin or get serious ingrown hairs from it. The final drawback to waxing is that you have to grow out a quarter inch of stubble before you can get waxed again—typically a wait of two to three *weeks.*

AT-HOME WAXING

There are lots of kits and products available at your local drug-store that will save you time and money by providing you with everything you need to wax yourself. These sound great in theory, but I have yet to meet a woman who has attempted to pull out her own pubic hair more than once.

SUGARING (OR STRINGING)

This hair-removal technique involves applying a sugar paste to the skin, then running a thick string over the area. The string removes the sugar, which has adhered to the hair, and pulls the hair out by the root. Those who have tried it say that it is less painful than waxing because the sugar sticks to the hair, not to the skin below it. When the sugar is removed, it doesn't pinch and pull at the skin the way wax does. Still, no matter what technique you use, having your hair ripped out at the root hurts. So you will be horribly surprised if you go in expecting a pain-free experience.

DEPILATORIES

Depilatories are chemicals you apply to your skin that will literally dissolve your unwanted hair right down into the follicle. Like home waxing kits, they are sold at drugstores, so you can use them in the privacy of your own home. They do work well for fine hair, like a light mustache. But forget depilatories for anything thicker and coarser—like your bikini area. Unless you have very fine hair down there, it won't completely dissolve. You'll then either have to do another application or switch to another method to get the rest of the hair off. This means shaving or re-treating chemically treated skin. Either way, it's time-consuming and can even be painful. I'm sure this alone seems bad enough, but there is one more drawback: smell. Depilatory creams have a horribly strong and unpleasant smell that no amount of added perfume can cover. The smell does go away once you wash off the cream, but the memory will linger in your traumatized nostrils for days.

SHAVING

Almost all dancers get rid of hair by shaving. All the other processes require a grow-out period of time that strippers don't have. For the beginner, I recommend getting a bikini wax done at a salon first, so you know where to shave when it starts to grow back in. If you don't want to subject yourself to a wax, try this instead: 1) Make sure you have a new razor with fresh blades and a pivot head. I like Gillette's triple-bladed Venus razor. 2) *Carefully* trim your hair with a small pair of scissors, as close to your skin as you possibly can. 3) Hop in the shower and apply a hair-softening shaving cream. Both Schick and Gillette make great-smelling shaving creams for women. If it's your first time using one, pick a cream made for sensitive skin to head off any possible reaction you might have. 4) Wait five minutes for your hair to soften, then start shaving. Remember: *Always shave in the same direction as the hair growth.* This will prevent razor burn and ingrown hairs. If for some reason you do get a couple of razor bumps, dab a little Tend Skin (available at drugstores and salons) or rubbing alcohol (yes, it hurts) on the area to help it heal faster.

Unfortunately, all hair-removal techniques—waxing, sugaring, depilatories, and shaving—tend to give you the occasional ingrown hair. It's certainly nothing that a good pair of tweezers and some Tend Skin won't solve. Dancers get nicks, bumps, ingrown hairs, and rashes all the time. When it's in a visible area, we usually cover it up with makeup. This is *not* something I would recommend for the civilian, because self-tanners, cover-ups, and bronzing powders really do exacerbate the problem. If you do find yourself getting a lot of ingrown hairs or razor burn or developing a rash, it's time to switch methods or stop altogether for a while until your skin can heal.

So now you know how strippers get their look, from top to bottom. Literally. To the average woman, the suggestions in this chapter might be a bit overwhelming. Hair extensions, a fake tan, false lashes, nail tips, and a Brazilian bikini wax do seem like a bit much put together. And you're right, it *is* a bit much. The classic stripper look is nothing if not over the top. For you, though, the key to your transformation is to take it slowly, do one thing at a time, and leave behind anything you don't feel completely comfortable with. If, after reading this chapter, all you do is change your brand of lip liner, you will at the very least have taken a step that will not only make you feel and look better but become hotter as well.

Here are some other books you might want check out: *Making Faces, The Art of Makeup,* and *Face Forward,* all by the late, great makeup artist Kevyn Aucoin. In all three books, he gives makeovers to women of all ages, weights, and ethnicities. He also tells you which products to use, along with easy-to-follow instructions on how to get the look for yourself at home.

EXERCISES

- Make a point of finding an extra five minutes a day that you can only use to pamper yourself. What is it that you usually don't have enough time to do? Brush your hair or style it any way except in a ponytail? Shave your legs or put on moisturizer? Slap on a coat of lipstick or mascara? If you actually clock yourself, you'll find that you can probably fit in all of the above.

- Set up an appointment to get anything done. Even if you are stone-cold broke you can afford a seven-dollar manicure. Don't do it yourself, even if you are a beautician by trade—it's too easy to mess up, too easy to quit, too easy to hear your hubby nagging you to bring a bag of chips over to the couch. The point of this exercise is to treat *you.*

- After you have carved some time into your schedule, try the Glama Pam makeup technique. Keep it private, so you have room to play around, make mistakes, change what you don't like, and keep what you do. With practice, it can take less than ten minutes to apply, and you'll have a new look to bust out any time you need a boost.

STRIPPER CHIC

STEP
FOUR

Now that you have the self-confidence, the attitude, and the look to go with them, you'll need something to wear. To inject a little stripper spice into your wardrobe, try some of the fashion tips in this chapter. You will learn:

- The top eight stripper looks
- What to wear over the top
- What goes underneath it all
- About strippers' favorite jewelry and accessories
- Practical applications for looking hot in real life.

OVER THE TOP

Strip clubs vary significantly in what they will allow you to wear. At some clubs around the country, dancers can wear hot pants and halters, jumpsuits, or even different kinds of costumes made out of interesting fabrics like leather, vinyl, or lace. In New York the options are surprisingly tame. Weekdays, dancers wear long spandex dresses; they have their choice of either long or short spandex dresses on the weekends. The type of spandex we wear must conform to code—it can't be sheer, and if there is lace, it can't be see-through. Vinyl, leather, and other "fetish" fabrics are also not permitted (unless, of course, you happen to strip at a fetish club). These little slips of spandex are expensive: Dancers pay between $150 and $250 for a dress with a matching G-string. And, mind you, this little piece of spandex is going to get stretched out, put on, and taken off hundreds of times over its short life. So while it might seem to the outsider that what a dancer wears is secondary to what she is willing to take off, that's actually not the case. Even for a dancer, the style and colors of the spandex she wears are important. They tell the customer a little about her. Whether she's conservative (yes, there are conservative strippers), liberal, materialistic, earthy, rich, or just looking to marry someone who is. Below are the eight basic dancer looks— the Bombshell, the Video Vixen, the Party Girl, the California Girl, the Uptown Girl, the Exotic, the Intellectual, and the Personal Trainer—and how to get them.

A stripper's look is defined by, uh, what she looks like . . . and to some extent, what she is capable of looking like. Within the boundaries of their specific look, strippers want to appeal to as many men as possible so they can make as much money as possible. For example, a dancer who is naturally something of an introvert might wear a black dress, with her hair in a ponytail or an upsweep, and accessorize with a pair of reading glasses. It's still a sexy look (it *is* black spandex, after all), but it's one that matches her personality and tells the customers a little about who she is (studious, smart, introverted). The same girl wouldn't feel comfortable in bright yellow ruffles or flamenco red. A dancer's look also helps the customer narrow down his choices. If he's out with a group of guys celebrating his bachelor party, he knows the studious introvert is not for him, because he's not looking to pay a girl for conversation. He's looking to do shot after shot until he's so hammered he has to rely on photographs to capture his memories. Instead, he'll choose the blond party girl in the hot-pink dress, because she is more suited to his personality that evening.

So dancers choose very carefully when shopping for a new dress for work. And with good reason—men, the poor creatures, for all their earning power, tend to frighten easily. Perhaps it's because they're so hell-bent on attaining world domination that they tend to feel threatened, especially by women (and even by strippers). Through decades of trial and error, dancers have come to know, in exacting detail, which looks work with men and which looks don't. So forget the latest fashion trends and what you see in magazines; the truth is that fashion is by women (or gay men) for women. Men's preferences don't change from season to season. A man will never decide that his look should be heavily influenced by the resurgence of mod, and he really doesn't want yours to be either. White lipstick looked bad in the sixties, and it looks bad now. If you happen to love it, then wear fashion when you dress to please yourself. When you want to please your man, follow the tips below.

THE TOP EIGHT STRIPPER LOOKS

The Bombshell

Bombshells are the dancers who, through some amazing combination of nature and technology, have a face and body that are so beautiful, one can only stand humbly by in awe. You know a bombshell when you see her by the dropped jaws and hushed voices that come over everyone when she passes by. Undoubted celebrity Bombshells are Catherine Zeta-Jones, Janet Jackson, and Michelle Pfeiffer. Because Bombshells are so beautiful, they don't need to rock any specific look—it all works on them. It's hard to say anything specific you can do to become a Bombshell, because so much of it depends on what you already have to work with. For example, Marilyn Monroe became a bombshell by dyeing her hair platinum, but only because she had an amazing face and body to start with. Madonna really looks no better or no worse as a blonde. And if you are Sarah Jessica Parker, you will not become Pamela Anderson by dyeing your hair platinum. For these reasons, unless you genuinely are a Bombshell (you'll know if you are) your best bet for this look is just to work within the confines of what God gave you. You'll feel more confident and look better too. *To get it:*

AT THE CLUB

The Look: Long hair overdue for a trim, Chap Stick, and mascara.

The Outfit: Basic black tube dress.

The Attitude: Whatever.

AT HOME

The Look: Messy ponytail, no makeup.

The Outfit: Baggy, ripped, or stained clothing falling off a perfectly toned, slender body.

The Attitude: Oh, God, they're all *looking* at me again.

The Video Vixen

Video Vixens are dancers who are just a hairsbreadth shy of being a Bombshell. They're still hotter than any woman you have ever seen in real life, mind you. They're just not the visions of walking perfection that Bombshells are. Vixens always look as if they have just stepped out of a music video—hence the name. The Vixen is a very done, if not overdone, look. Remember in chapter 3 when I said that having hair extensions, a fake tan, false eyelashes, nail tips, and a Brazilian bikini wax all at once might seem like a bit much? Well, Vixens have all of this *and* a bag of chips. Vixens think nothing of going to the local grocery store wearing a tube top, miniskirt, and platform mules—even if they're going out to buy tampons or diapers. *To get it:*

AT THE CLUB

The Look: Flawlessly done hair, makeup, and nails.
Fake *and* real tan.

The Outfit: White, orange, yellow, or gold dress with cutout *and* lace-up detailing. White patent-leather stilettos.

The Attitude: I'm, like, so totally hot! And you're so totally not!

AT HOME

The Look: Flawlessly done hair, makeup, and nails.
Fake *and* real tan.

The Outfit: Tight and bright. Strappy platform sandals.

The Attitude: I actually just cooked my family eggs in this outfit.

The Party Girl

You can spot a party girl by her big smile, raucous laugh, and the margarita clenched tightly in her white-knuckled hand. Think Tara Reid or Paris Hilton on a bender. Party Girls are Video Vixens who are too drunk to know that their mascara has smeared down to their chins. Because of their wild ways, Party Girls have a sexy, bad-girl quality to them that men *love.* There's something about the hot chick who can match you shot for shot and win. Sadly, Party Girls do face some health risks—such as retinal damage from constantly dilated pupils. And does anyone really want to see what Tara Reid or Paris Hilton are going to look like in ten years? Scary. *To get it:*

AT THE CLUB

The Look: Snarled hair, smeared mascara. Sparkly-tan skin.
The Outfit: Baby blue tube dress, worn inside out.
The Attitude: Will dance for booze!

AT HOME

The Look: Bed-head tousled the old-fashioned way.
The Outfit: Tight and bright with a cigarette burn hole in it.
  No shoes because you lost them.
The Attitude: Let's build a stripper pole in the kitchen!
  It'll be fun!

The California Girl

This is a girl who is stripping to pay for her reflexology course. She actually already has her bachelor's degree, but she wants to do something else so she can . . . you know . . . give something back. Californians are laid-back and radiate a friendly, approachable vibe from underneath their faded-orange spandex. *To get it:*

AT THE CLUB

The Look: Wavy, sun-kissed hair. Natural tan from spending the summer surfing.

The Outfit: Sunny, Left Coast colors or tie-dyes; low, matronly looking heels for comfort.

The Attitude: It's all about the love, isn't it?

AT HOME

The Look: Liberal dose of John Frieda's Ocean Waves; get a tan from gardening.

The Outfit: Snug-fitting baby tees and tanks; low-riding cargo pants and shorts. Sneakers or Birkenstocks.

The Attitude: Hey, dudes! How was your day at school?

The Uptown Girl

You can always tell an Uptown Girl because she wears her spandex like a power suit. If it weren't for the sparkles and the G-string, you would actually mistake her for a high-end real estate broker. Uptown Girls keep the cheese to a minimum by wearing their real jewelry to work. They spritz themselves with expensive, rare perfumes, and their five-inch stripper pumps are by Prada. *To get it:*

AT THE CLUB

The Look: Hot-rollered, sprayed hair. Soft, understated makeup that highlights the barest wisp of bronzer.

The Outfit: Loosely fitted spandex dress with a low cowl neck in white, periwinkle, or mint; chunky gold necklace, Manolo pumps.

The Attitude: If that's not a thousand dollars in your pocket,
you're *not* happy to see me.

AT HOME

The Look: Classy upsweep, color-coordinated makeup,
pale skin.

The Outfit: Nordstrom's finest.

The Attitude: Don't say it with words—say it with diamonds.

The Exotic

Some dancers choose to play into their ethnic background, whatever it is. I knew one girl whose grandparents were from Russia,
so she pretended to speak in a thick Russian accent, in the hopes
that men would take pity on her because of Russia's sad financial
state and give her more money.

This look varies widely depending on what your ethnic background is—or what it could be. For example, I don't have a drop
of Asian blood in me, but if I do my makeup right, even Asian
men think I'm mixed race. This is a fun look for me to try every
now and then when I'm feeling bored with the usual Vixen or
Intellectual looks. The key here is convenience. While I personally
thought Christina Aguilera looked fantastic when she changed her
look from underfed, generic-blond white girl to voluptuous, black-
haired Latina, the truth is that the poor girl had to have spent a
couple of hours a day tanning to get her skin that dark. And she's
half Ecuadoran! Sometimes, the amount of time or money you
need to put into a look makes it not worth it. If it is for you, here's
how *to get it:*

AT THE CLUB

The Look: Slicked-back ponytail, dark tan, cherry-red lips.
The Outfit: Red ruffles or off-the shoulder black.
The Attitude: I'm Ssssspicy!

AT HOME

The Look: Dark hair, purposeful ponytail. Fake tan, red-glossed lips.
The Outfit: Snug baby tee with *Latina* or *Asian Princess* emblazoned across the front. Low-rise, slim-fit, boot-cut jeans. Platform sandals.
The Attitude: Surprise, honey!

The Intellectual

The intellectual dancer shows that she's not like Bombshells, Vixens, or Party Girls by the serious look on her face and her refusal to smile. These girls are using their dancing dollars to pay for their undergrad degrees and hating every second of it. The Intellectual tries hard to look like she's not trying too hard. *To get it:*

AT THE CLUB

The Look: Hair in a ponytail. Fake, uneven tan. Strong, smoky eyes; deep bronze lips. Thick-rimmed correctional lenses.
The Outfit: Basic black in a simple, unfussy cut.
The Attitude: Get a dance or don't—I hate this stupid job anyway!

AT HOME

The Look: Messy hair from falling asleep on top of your textbook; makeup left over from the day before; tortoiseshell glasses.

The Outfit: Tight white tee; baggy jeans or sweats; sneakers.

The Attitude: Nutty professor.

The Personal Trainer

These are the girls (every club has one or two) who supplement their personal-training incomes by dancing. You can tell who they are by their painfully hard bodies, which they love posing and showing off. PT strippers look good, but dance badly—their taut muscles and stiff joints make every dance they do look like the Robot. Personally, I think that this look takes way too much damn work, but if you're willing to eat a lot of protein and work out for four hours a day, then go for it! *To get it:*

AT THE CLUB

The Look: Feminine, extra-blond, Miss America hair. Dark tan.

The Outfit: Supertight spandex, sturdy heels.

The Attitude: Get a dance, or I'll snap you like a twig.

AT HOME

The Look: Hot-rollered hair, extra-dark fake tan.

The Outfit: Hot-pink sports bra, skintight yoga pants, new sneakers.

The Attitude: Guess how much I can bench-press!

You can refer back to these eight basic stripper looks whenever you want to spice up your look or your life. As I've mentioned, I personally bounce between the Intellectual and the Vixen, depending on what mood I'm in, so there's no reason why you shouldn't try a couple on for size yourself. Now that you know the basics, here are a couple of other factors worth mentioning when it comes to putting together a hot look:

WHAT COLOR IS MY MONEY?

Dancers are notoriously superstitious about the colors they wear. Every girl has her "money colors"—the ones she wears because they seem to make more money for her than others. It might simply be that she has a personal preference for them, or it might be that they flatter her more than other colors. Both are good reasons for choosing the colors of the clothes you wear. Ask yourself: 1) Do you love the color? and 2) Does it look good on you? For example, I am a sucker for anything in baby pink or powder blue. Unfortunately, both these colors make me look like I'm surrounded by my coffin lining. To my eternal despair, I am a "fall" (you know, on the seasonal color wheel), so, sadly, only earth tones like rust, brown, gold, and olive green look good on me. To compromise, I'll wear pants or skirts in the colors I love, with a more neutral color on top that flatters my skin tone. What colors work on you also depends on your skin tone. Color Me Beautiful was really the first cosmetics company to analyze skin tone and recommend colors and products based on it. If you don't know, get your chart done by logging on to colormebeautiful.com. You can also go to the Prescriptives makeup counter at any department store. They will tell you (for free) what the underlying colors in your skin are. I am a yellow-orange, meaning that the base colors in my skin are—you guessed it—yellow and orange. You can then purchase Prescriptives makeup in colors designed to flatter your particular skin tone, or you can just study the colors they offer and buy a comparable, cheaper version at the local drugstore. Once you know what works best with your skin tone, you'll be able to figure out what *your* money colors are.

Men in the Mix

Men seem to have strong color preferences as well. So while you might love a particular color—chartreuse, for instance—your man might definitely not love it on you. Because of this, the colors you choose to wear are, in their way, more important than the cut. Below is a list of popular stripper colors and men's reactions to them. In general, men seem to like bright, cheerful colors or soft, pretty pastels. They like slutty colors like cherry red or hot pink only on slutty women (or on you when you're both at home role-playing Hugh Grant on a hooker hunt). They couldn't care less about subtle, understated shades like black, gray, navy, burgundy, or forest green.

In addition, colors send different messages depending on the cut and texture of the fabric, and even the time of day you wear them. For example, a cherry-red tube top would seem downright hookery by the light of day but could look simple and sexy at night. You'll stand out if you wear black during the day but fade into the wall if you wear it at night. Assuming that the former is your goal—wanting to stand out—I have broken down the best color choices for day and night. There's not a lot of magic to it.

The basic rule of thumb is go with darker colors during the day, and lighter, brighter ones at night.

If you want the cut or texture of the article of clothing to speak for you instead of the color, buy it in a day color. For example, a lemon-yellow velvet tube top would look garish even at night. Your best bet would be to choose the velvet tube top in black. The color is subtle, so the richness of the texture and the sexiness of the cut will stand out. If it's a more conservative cut, like a three-quarter-sleeve boatneck velvet top, then by all means, wear it in lemon yellow.

DAY COLORS	NIGHT COLORS
Black	White
Burgundy	Orange
Forest	Yellow
Navy	Cherry Red
Brown	Hot Pink
Gray	Chartreuse
	Bronze
	Gold
	Silver

Keep in mind that some colors and textures send a universal message—by day or by night.

ALWAYS SLUTTY

COLORS	TEXTURES
Cherry Red	Spandex
Hot Pink	Spandex with sparkles
Orange	Spandex with sequins

Yellow   Spandex with lace

Snakeskin print

Leopard or Tiger Print

And, surprisingly, all pastels

ALWAYS SAFE

COLORS	**TEXTURES**
Black	Cotton
White	Velvet
Periwinkle	Crepe
Mint	Wool
Buttercream	
Burgundy	
Bronze	
Forest	
Navy	

STYLE

The cut of the stripper dress is crucial. Most dresses are skintight, from top to bottom. So while this looks great on the one or two girls who supplement their personal-trainer incomes by stripping, it looks awful on the rest of the dancers, who, like most women, tend to be bottom-heavy. Still, whichever body type dancers have, and whether they're large breasted or small, most dancers choose dresses with a top that gives them some sort of boost. It is a top-*less* bar, after all. Below is an overview of the best ways to dress to emphasize your assets.

Best Bets for Busts

Any dress or top that has a built-in underwire bra gives the most lift. A popular style that offers a lot of push-up power is the bustier top. It's built to provide the support of a bra with the holding power of a corset, and it also has the full coverage of a tank or tube top. A close second for support is the built-in shelf bra. Many companies, such as Banana Republic and J. Crew, make their T-shirts and tank tops with shelf bras so you don't have to double up with a bra underneath.

The next most supportive are the halter styles, which lift and squeeze your boobs together, giving all but the AA's nice cleavage. Of course, if you do have small boobs, you can rock the sexiest look of all: braless. Nothing's hotter than a perky pair underneath a sporty baby tee or tank.

Whittle the Middle

To conceal a thick waist, dancers choose plunging necklines. The V-shape is standard, but a plunging cowl neck is flattering and elegant. A low neckline draws the eye upward and opens up your chest, making it look wider and your waist narrower. A classic example is the green Versace number Jennifer Lopez wore to the Emmys a few years ago. The plunging neckline and full skirt kept the focus on her T, not her A.

Another style dancers choose is the wrap dress. Wrap styles nip in the waist nicely while visually broadening your shoulders and chest. Both are good choices for whittling your middle and defining your curves.

Got Much Back

The great thing about having a larger backside is that it's versatile. Meaning, you can dress either to emphasize your round rump roast or to cover it up. If, like most of us, you want to cover it up, just wear something tight on top that boosts your ta-tas and whittles your middle, like a snug wrap shirt or bustier top. Pair it with a loose, flowing skirt or a pair of low-riding cargo pants and your little (or big) secret is completely hidden. If, on the other hand, you want to emphasize what you're packing in back, try something loose on top with some sexy tight low-riders. For dress-up, choose a high-necked, backless style that has a dramatic dip in back. Everyone will notice your delicious derriere and be begging you to "back that thang up."

For a more thorough analysis of your body type and problem areas, and to find out what clothes look good (or horrible) on you, check out the book *What Not to Wear* by Trinny Woodhall and Susannah Constantine. It's funny and well written; best of all, it uses pictures so you know exactly what they're talking about.

UNDERNEATH IT ALL

Since the whole point of getting dressed up is to get your man to undress you, let's get to the important part: what to wear when your clothes are off!

At my club, in addition to the mandatory G-string, we are also allowed to wear lingerie. Many dancers wear thigh-highs either with or without a matching garter belt. And some girls choose a complete ensemble—bra, garter belt, and thigh-highs. Some are even more adventurous and wear a matching corset to complete the look. When they give a dance, they first remove the dress, *then* the bra. Whatever the combination, lingerie worn underneath even a stripper dress is a sexy, welcome surprise. Imagine how much better the surprise will be for your man when he finds it underneath your power suit or Sunday best.

Bras

Push-up bras, like the Wonderbra and Miracle Bra, are available in a variety of styles and support. Most come with a little extra padding, which is removable if you are wearing it out on a manhunt and don't want to feel guilty of false advertising. Under a low-cut top, these bras will give even small-breasted women impressive cleavage. Choose a bra that offers fuller coverage if you plan on wearing it underneath a more conservative neckline, though. A demicup will cut you in half, giving you unattractive spillover and that weird four-boobed look.

STRIPPER TIPS!

- If you want mythic cleavage, of superhero proportions, choose a push-up bra one or two cup sizes smaller. For example, if you are a B-cup, try a bra that's an A-cup. The smaller cup size will force your boobs up and out, leading to Playmate-like curves.
- Any bra can be a Wonderbra; you just have to know how to trick it out. First, fasten the back clasp as tight as it will go. Then do the same with the shoulder straps. Next, take an old pair of shoulder pads or even some dress socks (you can use sport socks, but they

might be too bulky) and roll them up. Place each shoulder pad (or sock) to the far side of and slightly under each breast. The extra padding will push your breasts together and up, giving you some healthy cleavage and an extra boost. Obviously, don't do this if you think you're going to score with that hot guy you've had your eye on, because if a Wonderbra is looked down on as false advertising, having a pair of socks roll out as he takes off your bra is a downright bait-n-switch.

· Emergency cleavage: If you don't have any of the above tools at your disposal and you need cleavage stat, a strong adhesive like masking or duct tape works well too. First, make sure your skin is clean and dry and that you don't have any moisturizer on. Next, take the roll of tape and fix one end under (or as close to) your underarm as possible (but so that it won't be visible under your top). Unspool the tape across your chest. When you get to your breast, pull the tape tightly just underneath your nipple. This will look really weird, because you'll have boob coming out under *and* over the tape. Wind the tape across both breasts and secure it underneath your other underarm. You should now have eye-popping cleavage. If it's not an emergency, you can use this method with a strapless bra, assuming straps can't show—just pad out the spot where the tape cuts your breast with some tissues to give you a smooth line. If your top or dress is so skimpy that you can't even manage a strapless bra, but still want cleavage, many lingerie stores sell single-use "bras." They basically look like shoulder pads, with one side coated in adhesive so it will stick to your breasts. Smooth one of these over each boob, and you'll have support and coverage.

Braless

Nothing is quite as sexy as going au naturel. It's makes dressing more comfortable and easy. Obviously, this works best on women who have B-cups or under. Remember that episode of *Seinfeld* where Jerry's large-breasted ex-girlfriend (you know, the heir to the Oh Henry! bar fortune) wouldn't wear a bra? Not attractive. Large breasts need support. Likewise, small breasts that . . . this sounds so awful . . . sag also need the lift and coverage that only a bra can provide. But if you are blessed with small, high, perky breasts, make sure you dress to accentuate them. Most models (with the exception of the Victoria's Secret crew) are small-breasted, and dress to emphasize this. You can also take your cue from celebrities such as Cameron Diaz, Sarah Michelle Gellar, and Sarah Wynter, who are all unrepentantly flat.

Corsets

Imagine coming home after a long party. You and your man are in the back of the cab, making out passionately. He reaches his hand up the skirt of your dress. You hear his breath catch. *Hmmm, garter belt,* he thinks. He reaches up higher, and his eager fingers brush against smooth satiny fabric. *What is this?* he wonders. *A slip?* No, no, no. Nothing as uninspired as that. You have a much better surprise waiting for him.

Corsets are incredibly sexy, in so many ways. They nip you in and cover you up, completely taking any bloating issues you may have out of the picture. Plus, they make a sexy discovery when your man gets your dress off. And in any combination of sexy, slippery fabrics like satin, velvet, and lace, they feel good too.

Although nothing gives you more of an hourglass figure than the corset, nothing, unfortunately, leaves you as prone to fainting spells and organ displacement (?!) either. For these reasons, corsets are best left to sex-specific situations.

Look for corsets that have both a zip or hook-and-eye closure *and* a lace-up side or front as well. This allows for more give than lace-ups alone. Also, you'll be able to lace it yourself, so you won't have to ruin the surprise by asking your honey to come in and do it for you.

A WORD ABOUT COLOR: Corsets usually come in black or white. Black is sexy and looks extra badass in a corset. However, it can be a little too dominatrixy, especially in this kind of garment. This isn't a problem if it's something you or your man are into; otherwise, busting out a black lace-up corset might frighten him a little. Which isn't necessarily a bad thing.

White has an innocent virginal quality, especially in a corset, which I find balances out the garment's fetishy quality. Some lingerie shops also sell corsets in great colors and prints, like kimono red with gold and black dragons, or fetish fabrics like leather or rubber. Again, it's all about what you think you and your man might be into.

Bustiers

The bustier is a kind of bra-and-corset combination. These sexy, practical garments are perfect for wearing under dresses, or with outfits where you need to push some stuff out and pull other stuff in. Unlike corsets, they aren't bulky—most can be worn under the silkiest of fabrics. For these reasons, the bustier is your best bet if you want to get something new and sexy to wear for your man that you can actually use at times other than foreplay.

Choosing which one is right for you depends on what your needs are. Bustiers are practical, because you can wear them under many types of clothing, but their body-sculpting results are limited. The combination of a separate bra and corset allows for more control. You can boost your boobs higher and make your waist smaller with a combination than with just a bustier alone. So the real question for you is, which will you get more use out of? All three are great, fun, sexy items that will cause your man's jaw to drop—it's just a matter of what you like best.

Garter Belts

Garter belts drive men so crazy that I can't help but wonder, did they have the same effect way back when, before panty hose was invented? Because, let's face it, although panty hose is far more practical and useful than the garter belt–stocking combo, nothing—not even a big pair of flowered granny underwear—is less sexy than pantyhose. Garter belts are an easy, convenient way to sex up your look. Still, there are a couple of things to know if you want to work them right. For example, most garter belts latch around your upper waist. This is okay if you're slim; if you're not, the garter can cut you off, leaving you with a big stomach roll hanging over the top. And I'm sure I don't have to tell you that there's just about nothing that looks worse than a stomach roll hanging over the top of your garter belt. So if you're a bigger girl or are just feeling bloated, buy the garter one or two sizes bigger, so that it falls a few inches below your belly button. You'll still get coverage, and you won't risk rolls. The width of the garter belt is important too.

Narrow. Narrow garter belts are best on someone who is toned and taut. These provide the least coverage, and your skin will show above and below the belt. If you have a belly, this style will accentuate it. So avoid it unless, of course, that's the look you're going for.

Medium. Medium garters are great on any body type and provide total coverage below the belt. Some even provide a little support to help suck you in, if you need it. Just be careful, because these tend to have a bit of an old-fashioned or matronly look to them, which will quickly cool down an otherwise hot look.

Full. Full garters start at the waist and come down to cover all of your tum and most of your butt as well. They are fantastically sexy—they look like see-through lace miniskirts and are perfect for anyone who is self-conscious about her butt or thigh areas. If you are bigger, the extra fabric will cover you up and slim you down.

Stockings

Thigh-highs are great alone or with a garter belt. You can wear them to work or out on a date, and it'll make you feel sexy just knowing they're there. Most hosiery companies make them—but you'll have to try a few different brands to find the ones you like best.

STRIPPER TIPS!

You can actually wear thigh-highs to get a couple of different shaping effects.

- If you want to make your butt look smaller, buy thigh-highs one size larger than the size you normally wear and pull them up as high as they will go. The extra fabric will cover your upper thighs (visually the widest point on most women), making your butt appear smaller.
- If you want your butt to look *bigger*, buy stockings one size smaller than the size you normally wear. Or you can buy stockings that are designed to come up just over the knee or to midthigh. The lower height will visually shorten the length of the leg, making your butt and thighs look curvier.

Thongs and Panties

Thongs (or G-strings) are not for the faint of heart. For those who have never worn one, let me tell you right now: Thongs are not comfortable. Do not listen to any skinny supermodel who says that she loves them and can't even feel them. You *can* feel them, it's just that during the day you are so absorbed doing other stuff that you don't think about them. But, as with a wedgie, if you stop for two seconds you *will* be driven nuts by the inability to get your underwear out of your ass. Having said that, I have to add that there are few lingerie items that men feel as passionately about as the thong. After all, it is how Monica Lewinsky snagged the President—flashing a flowered pair of grandma panties wouldn't have done it. Make no mistake, it was the thong that captured his imagination. And for good reason. Thongs are flattering. It doesn't matter how big your butt is, a thong will make it look better. There was even a Top Ten song about them by the R&B artist Sisqó—called, fittingly enough, "Thong Song." Although they're not made of much, thongs come in a surprisingly wide variety of styles. The best one for you depends on your preferences and body type.

THE CLASSIC

This is the traditional thong that most strippers wear at work. Usually made of lined spandex, it provides full coverage for what's underneath. The crotch part is wide enough that you won't be in danger of accidentally flashing anyone, no matter how bendy you are, and the back is generally about an inch wide. What makes this thong classic is its super-high-cut leg. On most women, the sides sit comfortably right at your waist. This style looks good on everyone, but it works best on women who are thick-waisted, because the deep V line of the thong visually narrows your waist. On the downside, these cuts don't work well with garter belts, because the sides will come up higher than the waistline of the garter belt, which just looks weird.

HIGH-RIDERS

The main difference (besides fabric) between the high-rider thong and the classic thong is that high-rider's fabric stretches straight across your stomach, instead of dipping down in a deep V. Because of its high cut, this style still nips in your waist, but it also provides excellent coverage if you are self-conscious about your stomach. Another plus is that there are a variety of backs to choose from. Some people think that the less fabric in your butt crack, the less you feel it. For this reason. Calvin Klein's classic thong (it has nothing but a string—literally—in back) is a popular choice. Personally, I think that the *softer* the fabric in your butt crack, the less you will feel it. So I like Christian Dior's thongs and Victoria's Secret Body by Victoria thongs. The microfiber fabric is so soft you truly do not know it's there.

LOW-RIDERS

I find low-rise panties much sexier than high-cut, because they let the eye travel uninterrupted from shoulder to hip, with nothing to see except your gorgeous skin. For this reason, low-riders also make you look curvier. I also prefer them under a garter, because the sides don't ride up. Low-riders, like high-riders, come with different width backs, so choose whichever you find most comfortable.

STRIPPER TIPS!

I have saddlebags. If you are so blessed to have lived your life without having them or knowing what they are, let me fill you in. Saddlebags are the unfortunate fat deposits that sit at the top of your thighs, on your lower hip. On me, like on many women, saddlebags cause a hellish silhouette. It's a sort of double-hipped effect: My waist goes in, then my upper hips go out; then my middle hips go in, and my lower hips go out again. On me, like on many women, my saddlebags are actually the widest part of my body, making traditional hip measurements for clothing irrelevant. For those of us so cursed, low-rider thongs make a flattering panty choice. The sides of low-riders tend to rest squarely on the middle hip, filling it in with fabric. Visually, it gives the curve of your hip a smoother line. And when you pair low-riders with thigh-highs, you won't even remember you have saddlebags.

BOY-CUT

Boy-cut thongs are incredibly flattering because they give the most coverage. They're also really comfortable, since the actual thong part doesn't run up the entire length of your butt—it's just an inch or two of fabric before it meets up with the rest of the short. They feel better than most other types of thongs because with less fabric in your butt, there's less pull, so you won't have that vague feeling of having a wedgie you can't get rid of.

Other Underwear

Thongs are not your only option. Men do seem to prefer them but, like anything else, only in moderation. If you are a thong-only kind of gal, shake it up a bit with a pair of boy-cuts or bikinis. Men also love the innocent, fresh look of a pair of clean white cotton underwear.

Caution!

If you are underwear shopping and do not want to wear a thong, just make sure you stay away from any kind of grandma panties. For the most part, you'll know them on sight: big and ugly, with yards of fabric starting at your high waist and covering all the way down to your thigh. However, underwear makers have gotten clever in their attempts to foist grandma panties on the unsuspecting shopper. These insidiously disguised items now hang on the rack next to sexy, fuller-cut bras. They're made in shiny, satiny fabrics with lacy details so that, hanging on the rack, they look just like ordinary underwear. Do not fall for this! Do not make the mistake of buying a pair because they look cute on the rack! Take the panties away from the alluring colors of the dazzling display and fully inspect them before you purchase them. They might look satiny, but are they really polyester? They might be lacy, but is it the same kind of lace you see trimming doilies at your spinster aunt's house? When in doubt, simply ask: Is there enough fabric here to rig a sail? If the answer is yes, they're grandma panties.

SHOES

There are few things in life that women feel as passionately about as shoes. Shoes are like lipstick—easy on and off, with the power to make or break any outfit. They're what make cheap suits look good, and good suits look cheap. Shoes are important.

At the club where I work, shoes need to have a heel at least three inches high and be in the classic stiletto style. While that's an incredibly sexy shoe, it's always good for a girl to have options. To get the total stripper look, try these:

Stilettos. Stilettos are the all-time fuck-me shoe. Which is good, because they're so painful to wear for any extended period of time that they're best reserved for sex. Strippers wear theirs five inches high, but it's safer for the civilian to go with three-inch heals

Pumps. Pumps have sleek stiletto styling without the nosebleed height. While you technically need some height in order for the shoe to be called a pump, you can find this sleek style with heels as low as one inch. Obviously, the higher you go, the sexier they look, but if you need to compromise, pumps up to three inches can be worn for work or for play.

Platforms. Platform shoes are the single best thing to come out of the seventies. For dancers at clubs where there's a choice, platform heels are the only way to go. The most popular are the open-toed, sandal type, with a five-inch heel and a three-inch platform under the ball of the foot. These give you amazing height (I dare you to put on a pair and not feel like a supermodel) and crucial cushioning. Platforms are so comfortable that most women feel like they could walk around in them all day. However, because it's a bold shoe with a bold look, it's best if you save them for going out dancing at a club or going to the club to dance.

Boots. Boots are really, really sexy—and if you have the right pair, you don't need lingerie at all. My personal preference for total male domination are thigh-high patent-leather boots with a platform stiletto heel. They come in lots of colors, black (badass), white (futuristic), red (devilish), hot pink (Playboy Playmate). The only drawback is that you cannot leave the house wearing them. If you don't understand why, try to imagine actually doing it. You cannot slip on a pair of patent-leather thigh-high boots for a quick run to the grocery store for some milk and margarine. These boots will never leave your bedroom (except maybe on Halloween—and even as part of a costume they'll cause a scandal).

ACCESSORIES

Men love jewelry, and they should be encouraged to give it to us at every opportunity. Here are strippers' top choices:

Earrings

Hoops. The hands-down sexiest earring is the hoop. Go smaller if you're conservative, as big as you can handle if you're feeling frisky. Just make sure they're smaller than your actual head. Gold and silver look summery and sexy, while cubic zirconia–encrusted hoops add a touch of old Hollywood Marilyn glamour.

Studs. The next sexiest style is the stud. Whether they're diamond, pearl, or simple gold or silver, studs act as punctuation marks for your face.

Dangly. Earrings that dangle can be sexy for a night out—but they're difficult to dance in because they tend to get tangled up in long hair. Ditto for sex.

Necklaces

Chokers. This is the sexiest style you can get. Chokers frame the face and define your neckline. They also have a little bit of a naughty S&M feel to them, which is a fun way to keep guys guessing about who's the boss.

Crosses and Other Religious Symbols. These are hot—because they add a touch of good girl to any bad-girl outfit or activity. Just remove them before you do anything you'll need to go to confession for.

Initials. Another style that's popular is the nameplate necklace, which literally spells out your first name in gold or, depending on your net worth, diamonds. A subtler, flirty version of this is the initial pendant, a simple gold or silver chain with your first initial dangling from it. This is a great piece of jewelry to break the ice, because cute strange men will be compelled to come up to you and try to guess what your first name is. Just make sure you save these for when you're actually seeking out attention from the opposite sex; otherwise they'll drive you crazy.

Lariats. Lariats are sexy because they drop straight down between your breasts, drawing all attention in that direction, like an arrow on a road map. Pair the lariat with a low-cut blouse or dress to heighten the effect.

Bracelets

Tennis. Uptown Girl dancers and all other well-kept women always wear the classic diamond tennis bracelet. Sometimes wearing something so expensive feels sexy. If you can't understand why, imagine having ten thousand dollars' worth of diamonds on your wrist right now. Pretty good, huh?

Bangles. Bangles add an earthy, gypsy feel to any look, which most men find sexy. Whether they're gold, silver, brass, or even rubber, bangles emphasize your gestures with their movement and cheerful jangling sound. As a bonus, their oversize dimensions slim down the look of the arm.

Cuffs. Leather wrist and arm cuffs have become popular recently; they have a bad-girl rock-and-roll edge. These pieces, like chokers, also have a bit of an S&M feel to them, which is always fun. Cuffs fit snugly, so they look best on skinny wrists or arms.

Watches

Every stripper wears a watch so she'll know when her hour in the VIP room is over. Feminine bracelet styles are always nice, but I personally prefer my Baby-G Dolphin sport watch. I like the way its rugged look contrasts with my otherwise ultragirly stripper look. It adds a touch of surprise, of the unexpected. You can do the same by pairing a delicate watch with a sporty outfit, or a big chunky boy-style watch with an evening dress.

Rings

Rings are tricky. Wear the wrong kind on the wrong finger, and an otherwise available woman will look taken. Wear only one, and the ring will look special. Wear too many, and you'll look like a gangsta rapper. Here are a couple of tips to help you choose which rings and how many are right for you:

- Contrary to popular opinion, an engagement-style ring will not stop men from hitting on you. In fact, they'll actually be more likely to approach you because you'll seem "safe." You're not out on a manhunt, because you've already got one. Wear this style of ring on the ring finger of your left hand the next time you and your girls go out, and you'll see what I mean. (When the guy who approaches you asks about the ring, tell him you wear it only to weed out the riffraff—or that your beloved grandmother gave it to you.)

- Gold has to be really artsy or really expensive; otherwise it just looks cheap. To keep this from happening, try wearing the ring on an unconventional finger—your pinkie, index, or thumb, for example.

- Silver rings and silver rings with stones have a funky, hippie quality to them. Feel free to pile on (two to a finger if you want) as many as you feel comfortable with.

Body Jewelry

Everyone predicted that the body-piercing craze would fade away, leaving millions of punctured twenty-somethings wondering what the hell they'd been thinking. Much to the chagrin of parents everywhere, body piercing has not lost its popularity. In fact, it's become rather commonplace. While a large percentage of strippers have multiple piercings—eyebrows, noses, lips, nipples, navels, *and* nether regions—most strip clubs do not allow strippers to wear body jewelry at work. The reason is that most men are still pretty conservative. So even though Christina Aguilera might boast about her diamond nipple studs, most men really don't want to see them.

Accessory Style

Sometimes it's not so much what you wear as what you wear it with. Even strippers do the less-is-more thing when it comes to accessories. I always wear the same exact pieces when I dance, no matter what the color and cut of my dress. My personal faves are medium-size gold hoop earrings, a three-tier pearl choker, and a simple gold-band thumb ring. But while this combo seems to work well for me inside the club, I know it would be a bit dramatic in real life. It's best to play around and see what you feel comfortable with. Add a choker or a different pair of earrings. You'll be surprised at the difference a little change can make.

So now you have a complete breakdown of all the options available to help your sexy self get the stripper silhouette. Here's how you put it all together:

HOW TO CREATE THE STRIPPER SILHOUETTE

At the club, we're limited as to what we can wear. Of course, there are some things we are allowed to wear but don't because they become too unwieldy in the fast, "take it off, put it on again" environment of the club. For example, bras make me feel incredibly sexy when I get to dance in them, but for practical reasons they just don't work. Basically, the time spent hooking up your bra is time you could have been doing another dance—and making another twenty dollars. Outside the confines of the club requirements, my dream dance outfit is this: lacy push-up bra, large (skirt-style) garter belt, thigh-highs, and heels. In white. I love white because it makes me feel feminine, innocent, and girly. It brings back a sense of fun to the dance. I like the silhouette this combination gives me: The push-up makes my C-cups look higher and perkier, and the skirt-style garter shows off my relatively toned tummy but covers up my very untoned ass. The thigh-highs hide the worst offenders—my saddlebags—and the heels give me so much extra height that I look supermodel-slim. This is what makes me feel sexy.

Every now and then, I also like to rock a black satin corset with a matching G-string. I love how little it makes my waist look, and how big and curvy my boobs and butt look in contrast. The black color makes me feel tough and in charge, and it's a look and an attitude that my man appreciates too. It's important for you to try stuff on and find out what makes you feel comfortable, because that's what you'll feel sexiest in. For instance, classic lingerie is not the only way to go. There are lots of other options out there. Some women like fetishwear and feel sexiest in a sparkly gold leather thong or a rubber dress. If this is something you've thought about but never really explored, the Internet is a great place to start. It's private, you can order stuff online, and in some cases you can have things made to order. For example, if you go type the words "exotic dancewear" into any search engine, you'll get thousands of hits for boutiques that stock the latest in everything from run-of-the-mill spandex and lace to leather, vinyl, rubber, and more. Most of these sites offer all of these styles in plus sizes too, so if you're a bigger girl, don't think this stuff is out of reach.

PRACTICAL APPLICATION

For those with careers or full-time jobs, finding little ways to spice up your look is easy, because dressing up, wearing makeup, and looking sharp (no matter how casual the office) are all part of the routine. For the rest of us—many of whom are stay-at-home moms who work only part-time—the cost-benefit scale of looking hot is hopelessly skewed. For example, a day in my life goes like this: 4:00 A.M.: Wake and get my cranky son milk, in the hope that he'll fall back to sleep. 6:00: Wake and get my cranky son milk in the hope that he'll fall back to sleep again. 7:00: Wake up, plop son in front TV to watch *Dragon Tales* or *The Wiggles* while I make coffee. 7:15: Plop self in front of TV while I burn my mouth trying to drink my too hot coffee; wait for coffee to cool and attempt to wake up by force of will alone. 8:00: Try to entice my son into his high chair to eat breakfast. 8:30: Forcibly remove son from in front of TV and place in high chair to eat breakfast. 9:00: Brush teeth, get son and self dressed. 9:30: Go to local grocery store to pick up the favorite cereal that we were out of at breakfast. 10:15: Arrive back home and put groceries away. 10:30: Give my son a snack. 11:00: Leave for playground. 12:30: Return home from playground, eat lunch. 1:00: Watch *Dora the Explorer* ("Dora! Dora! Boots! Dora! Boots! *Teevee Mommy teevee Dora now!*"). 1:30: Quiet storytime while I try to settle my son in to nap. 2:00: More quiet storytime as I still try to settle my son in to nap. 2:30 to 4:00: Nap. 4:00: Watch *Dora the Explorer* ("Dora! Dora! Boots!

Dora! Boots! *Teevee Mommy teevee Dora now!*") again. 4:30:
Snack. 5:00: Go for long walk. 6:30: Make dinner. 7:00: Eat dinner. 7:30: Play outside in the yard, weather permitting. 8:00:
Crayon, marker, and crafts time. 8:30: Bath time. 9:00: Storytime.
9:30: More storytime. 10:00: Lights out. 10:30: Son finally, finally
falls asleep.

Now, you might look at my schedule and mockingly think that
I have plenty of time during the day to get the things done that I
need to, like, oh, for instance, taking a shower. You might even
think I'm being lazy—after all, I could easily fit in a TaeBo video
workout or something while he naps. And you might actually be
right. But I have a shameful confession: The task of keeping a
two-year-old educated and entertained for over fifteen hours a day
is so consuming that I just don't care. Make no mistake: I want to
care. I just don't.

My husband, poor soul, only sees me in the morning, when
we're both equally ugly, and then again at night, after I've had
such a full and exhausting day that the dead-last thing I want to
worry about is whether my jeans make my butt look good. I am
sad to say that even though as a dancer I am deeply committed to
looking as hot as I can, as a wife and mother my apathy runs a
mile deep and wide. Here's another shameful confession: I am a
sweat suit addict. Not those cute, velour, Juicy Couture or Enyce
combinations; no, I'm talking seven-dollar Wal-Mart specials—
Hanes, baby, Hanes!

Since I have a toddler, I know that anything I wear is going to
get splattered with, well, anything he can get his hands on. And
then there's the fact that I personally happen to be a spaz. Between
the two of us, it just makes the idea of wearing nice (i.e., expensive) clothes seem stupid. Plus, there's the fact that I love sweat-

pants. I love the thick, cottony texture and the abnormally low crotch, evocative of MC Hammer pants. And, as one of those always-cold-even-if-it's-eighty-degrees-out people, I love their enduring comfort and warmth. Of course, I look like a train wreck in them. A big Magic-Marker-and-SpaghettiOs-stained train wreck. But sometimes it's too hard to resist wearing something that feels as cozy and comfy as a down blanket on a Sunday morning.

Unfortunately, while wearing sweats does enhance the shelf life of my nice clothes, it does nothing to enhance my sex life with my husband. It's not that he cares what I wear—he's as happy to peel me out of my stained sweats as he is to peel me out of a tailored suit. It's just that it's hard for me to feel sexy when, in a moment of passion, my husband lifts up my shirt and out fall the few Cheerios that got glued to me while I was trying to feed my son breakfast. So while it's very important to me that I feel comfortable in my everyday life, it's also important that I feel sexy and confident. For these reasons, then, although it's always a struggle, I make the extra effort.

Not everyone loves sweats as much as I do. A few lucky souls among us have made it through motherhood in chinos, sweater sets, and pearls. But every single one of us commits a crime against our inner hottie at least once a month by wearing the most hideous article of clothing of all: *safety panties.*

Most women have two kinds of underwear: the sexy, silky kind they wear when they think that they're going to get a li'l somethin', and the big, stained, holey kind they wear the rest of the time. I'm as guilty as the next—only I bought all my comfortable cotton undies in black, so they've aged a little more gracefully. The problem is that having too many comfortable pairs of underwear can lead to laziness. And really, who wants to put on a thong when there's a perfectly good—if not overworn—pair of flowered cotton grandma panties just sitting there?

If You Were in an Accident ...

Women *do* think this way. How many times in your life have you declined your man's advances because you haven't taken a shower or have a few days' stubble on your legs, pits, or bikini area? How many times have you turned down sex with someone you were just getting to know because you didn't want him taking off your skirt only to discover a huge pair of grandma panties? Relaxing your diligence in wearing presentable skivvies leads only to less nookie. Your mother's advice about always putting on decent panties (you know, in case you're in an accident, your doctor won't have to see your nasty old underwear) is vitally important . . . to your sex life. Here are some more reasons for wearing nice underthings: Putting on an old pair of underwear is a subconscious way of eliminating the option of sex. Why? Because no woman wants her man seeing her in a pair of GPs. On the flip side, wearing sexy underwear subconsciously keeps the possibility of sex open, even if, like me, you put them on underneath a pair of Hanes sweats. Plus, sexy underwear makes you feel sexy. Every time you see them or think about them, you think about sex. This is a good thing! Thinking about sex and thinking about yourself as a sexy mama leads to feeling more comfortable with your body and your sexuality.

Even the small reminders, like a sexy pair of panties, keep you focused on your goal of unleashing your inner hottie. Dressing for the possibility of sex, whether or not there is a man in your life, will make you feel sexy.

EXERCISE: THE WILL TO BE HOT

In most dependency-recovery programs, the first step is admitting you have a problem. The truth is, you would not be reading this book right now if some teensy tiny part of you didn't know that your use of baggy sweats or big, white T-shirts had become a problem. On some level, you know you are dependent on ugly, unflattering clothes, and you also know that this dependency has become unhealthy for you. Sure, you started out with only casual use: borrowing your husband's sweatshirts here, picking up an extra pair of overalls "just in case" there. But it snowballed, didn't it? Your casual use of unflattering clothing became an addiction because you liked the way they made you feel. And they felt good, didn't they? So snug, warm, and comfortable. As opposed to the tight fits and the pinching and pulling of today's "fashion." Until one day, they just took over your wardrobe. Suddenly you realized that you didn't recognize any of the other clothes in your closet because it had been so long since you'd worn them. You'd grown so accustomed to looking casual (i.e., slobby) that looking good just didn't look so good to you anymore. Friends and relatives made comments like "Oh, you look so pretty when you dress up," in attempts to let you know just how far you'd slid. But what they said didn't matter, did it? Because you'd stopped caring. And what's worse is that you no longer *cared* that you didn't care.

STEP 1. Well, it's okay now. It's going to be all right. *You are taking the first step.* Today, you have made tremendous progress by just admitting you have a problem. From now on, you will think twice before reaching for a sweatshirt or your husband's baggy white tee. You will be able to recognize the fact that you are making a *choice* in putting on grandma panties instead of sexy lace. You needn't take any action yet. For now, it's enough to become aware of the choices you make.

STEP 2. The next time you are getting dressed and recognize that you are reaching for your old GPs, stop where you are and ask yourself if you have a comfy pair of lacy boy-cuts you can wear instead. It's okay if you don't have anything else to put on. It's also okay if you decide that you want to wear the GPs and not the lacy boy-cuts. The road to recovery is long and slow, and it's marked with backslides and pain. But have faith, and trust that someday soon you will put the sweatshirt back in your drawer forever.0

Finding ways to stripperfy even the most casual look is easy—have you ever seen an episode of *Baywatch*? These are people whose work uniform is a *swimsuit*. But you'd never catch Pamela Anderson or Yasmine Bleeth hanging around off duty in a pair of Hanes Her Ways. Here are some easy ways to sex up your casual look:

IF YOU WEAR . . .	**REPLACE WITH . . .**
Baggy sweatshirts	Slim cotton sweaters
Hoodie jackets	Fitted zip cardigans or fleece
Big white tees	Fitted or baby tees
Random-logo tees	Flirty-logo tees (tees with words like *Spoiled* on them)
Sweatpants	Yoga pants
Baggy jeans	Fitted low-riders (with stretch for comfort)
Baseball caps	Baseball caps (men love them)

Heels

Remember that shoes can make or break a look. Even a high-buttoned collar and roomy pants will look slutty if you wear them with patent-leather pumps. You can make Laura Ashley herself look like a ho if you strap on a pair of Jimmy Choos. If you want to tart yourself up, just throw on a pair of sexy platform sandals with your low-riding jeans or cargoes. In the winter, a pair of high boots looks great with denim skirts or even corduroys.

EXERCISE: CHOOSE YOUR WEAPONS

Go to your nearest Victoria's Secret (or wherever they sell the stuff you're looking for). I like Vickie's, because they have a large selection and big, comfortable (pink!) dressing rooms. You can spend all day in there trying on outfits and figuring out what looks best on you. The only thing you aren't allowed to try on is any kind of thong. This isn't necessarily a problem—you can return it after you take it home if it doesn't fit, and your account will be fully credited. In addition, Vickie's policy is to "damage out" any underwear that gets returned, so it's nice to know, for hygiene reasons, that no one else has tried them on. Be careful, though: Vickie's stuff tends to run small, so if you're between sizes, opt for the larger one. Panties that are slightly too large still look and feel fine, but panties that are too snug are unwearable.

EXERCISE: GET READY!

Make sure you are alone. You really, *really* don't want the kiddies walking in on this one.

Next, choose your weapons (i.e., pieces of lingerie to wear for your man); you need break them in. Put on the outfit you have chosen, along with the shoes that go with it. You don't need to do your hair and makeup, but if it will help get you in the mood, knock yourself out. Now put on a CD you love. It should have *at least* three songs in a row you feel comfortable dancing to. Finally, use the steps to the basic striptease that you learned (and hopefully have practiced) in chapter 1. However, don't actually take anything off. This isn't a dry run of the dance you'll be doing for your man. Don't worry about how good you look or how well you move. Just begin to dance, slowly. Use a mirror if you'd like. Give yourself a chance to get used to the look and feel of your lingerie. Give yourself a chance to get used to dancing in high heels. Most importantly, give yourself a chance to feel like the hottie you are.

NOTE: HOW NOT TO TRIP: If you did the above exercise and now want to try taking your clothes off, here's how to do it without tripping and falling. Remove your dress (or hot pants or bottoms) and let it fall to the floor at your feet. Use one hand to lean on the arm or the back of the chair where your man will be sitting when you give the dance. Leaning on the chair, lift one foot and, making sure it is not tangled in your discarded fabric, place it outside the dress. Next, do the same with the other foot. Once you are free, you can bend over and pick it up, or do what dancers do and simply kick it out of your way. This may sound simple enough, but it's actually pretty tricky in five-inch heels, so it's worth it to practice a couple of times for safety's sake.

THE BIG TEASE

STEP
FIVE

Strip clubs are like exotic buffets where men recline in cushy chairs like fat, happy pashas surveying the feast. They see something they like, ring a bell, and it is brought to them on a gilded tray. Beautiful, barely dressed women happily cater to every whim and desire. Which brand of vodka, sir? Which kind of cigar? A brunette with small breasts? Certainly, sir. As you see, the stripper fantasy is a rather powerful one for men, one that they are willing to spend lavishly to fulfill. At the club where I work, a customer pays a $30 cover charge just to walk in the door. The mandatory coat check is an additional $10, and if he wants a bottle of Bud, it will cost him another $12, not including the tip. A three-minute lap dance from one of the entertainers will run him $20. One hour in the Champagne Room with said entertainer will cost him $550 (a $150 entrance fee, $400 for the dancer's time), and no, a bottle of champagne is not included. That will set him back an extra $150 for the house brand, or up to $1,000 for special reserve Cristal.

So what do men get, other than fantasy, as a return on their investment? The answer is, a whole lot of nothing. You see, at my club there is no "lap" in the lap dance. I use this term because it is the most common, but what dancers at my club actually do for their three-minute song is a table dance. We are required by law to stand a certain distance away from the customer while giving a dance. A dancer who touches a customer (even accidentally) while giving a dance risks being fined, suspended, or fired. A customer who in any way touches a dancer risks being pummeled on the sidewalk by a muscle-bound bouncer. At no time may a dancer sit on a customer's lap, whether she has her dress on or not. This will result in automatic termination. So let go of what you learned from watching *Showgirls*. Men don't come to strip clubs for the "happy ending"; they come for the big tease.

WIN VALUABLE CASH AND PRIZES!

My club seats about five hundred people, and there are usually around one hundred girls working each night. We make money by going up to each and every customer (sometimes several times) and asking them if they'd like a dance. It sounds easy, but the truth is that it can be quite hard. As I mentioned in chapter 1, every dancer, no matter how big her boobs, blond her hair, or tan her skin, will be rejected hundreds of times over the course of an eight-hour shift. The rejection alone is bad enough—but here's some math: If a full club sat 500 people one night and you earned $500 dollars, you did only twenty-five dances. That means that the other 475 people you asked said no to you. It's really pretty horrible if you think about it. Can you imagine going to a bar or club and asking every available man if they'd like to take you out? What's worse is that as dancers, we're not even looking for that kind of commitment. We're asking these men if they'd like to see us *naked,* and they still say no.

Still, five hundred dollars a night is a whole lot of money. And the possibility of earning a lot more is always present. I have heard of girls who have made five, six, even ten *thousand* dollars in one night. Sometimes, thoughtful customers even give us gifts—boob jobs, laptops, Cartier watches, Coach handbags, or designer threads. You might think that dancers can get these kinds of cash and prizes only by sleeping with their customers. Actually, the opposite is true: We're able to get all this stuff only by *not* sleeping with our customers. Why? Because of one simple principle: Men want what they can't have. For various reasons explained in this chapter, the dancer-customer relationship is like the infatuation phase you go through when you first start dating someone. It's similar to that oh-so-golden period where a guy is willing to do anything for you. Get reservations to the hottest restaurant in town? Done. Rub your feet and paint your toenails? Sure. Pretend to like your cat? On it. Listen with fascination to your endless complaints about your coworkers? Absolutely. It's only after that infatuation turns into a "relationship" that he shushes you when the TV's on so he can hear the game. The dancer's challenge, then, is basically to get as much money out of her customer as possible before he falls out of infatuation with her.

THE GENTLE ART OF MANIPULATION

Some people may think that the following advice is manipulative, to which I say: So what? *Manipulation* has become an unnecessarily dirty word in relationship-speak. It's true that no one wants to feel used or taken advantage of. And no one really deserves to be, either. I'm not talking about manipulation in some Machiavellian it's-better-that-your-partner-fears-you-than-loves-you sort of way. The way strippers manipulate their customers is by speaking and acting in a way that will get the best possible results. For a stripper this means cash; for you, it might mean putting some sparks back into your sex life.

This sounds cold and calculating, but it really isn't. Everyone knows you get better results by speaking *nicely* to the airline agent who just sent your luggage to Thailand then by screaming and cursing at her. Likewise, when you're at work you behave one way around your boss and another around your clients. Is this manipulative? Sure. Does this mean you are using or taking advantage of your boss or clients? Well, no. When men enter a strip club, they know exactly what they're there for. They know that they are going to spend money, they know how much, and they know on whom. Strippers have simply learned, through their night-to-night interactions with men, what to do to maximize their chances of getting some of that money. These techniques can be handy if you've found that for whatever reason your current approach to getting what you want isn't working or is being met with resistance by your partner.

WHAT DO YOU WANT?

I have broken down the components of what a dancer does each night, both inwardly and outwardly, to cause customers to fall madly into infatuation with her (and make as much money as possible). You can use them to get your man reinfatuated with you. These techniques can be used separately to boost your self-confidence and keep your man on his toes. Or, better yet, put all of them together to get him to buy you a new car.

The first and most important step is the preparation. In "Creating the Buzz" you will learn to create a buzz of energy within and around yourself; then you can draw off this energy any time you need a shot of self-confidence.

PREPARATION: CREATING THE BUZZ

When a man first likes you, he thinks (rightly so) that you are the most beautiful, interesting, special woman on the face of the earth. And it's hard not to feel that way yourself when you have this wonderful man thinking so highly of you. Although your man certainly still feels this way about you, how long has it been since you've felt this way about *yourself*? The first thing dancers do after they put on their makeup and get dressed is to get in touch with this feeling of being powerful and amazing, in order to create a buzz. You most often see the term *buzz* in gossip columns about celebrities. It means that they are hot and sought after, that they have a lot of potential. If the celebrity were a racehorse, they'd be the horse on which you'd put all your money.

Plug It In

You'll need to find a quiet place. These don't actually exist in a strip club, so anywhere—including a restroom stall—will do just fine. Take a few deep breaths. Center yourself and gather your energy. Then think: What are your special qualities? Are you pretty? Smart? Funny? Good at math? Have nice big toes? Use whatever works. It doesn't matter that there are other women out there with nice or (gasp!) even *nicer* big toes. These lovely toes are yours, and they're part of what makes you special. Allow yourself to feel fantastic about your big toes, and all of your special qualities. Allow this feeling to fill you up until your body can't contain it, and it spills over, radiating light and heat. Strippers reach deep within themselves to find this essence, like a firefly's glow, with the expectation that they will find a customer attracted to that glow.

You can do this in a million different ways. For example, imagine that you have been officially certified the most beautiful woman in the world. They took you to a lab, ran some tests, and found that you are without a doubt the standard for universal beauty. You have been interviewed, photographed, pursued. Actors, models, even Prince William (poor dear) all call and text-message you what seems like every other second. Or you can pretend that you are a hot female celebrity. What is it like to be Britney Spears? How would you feel right now if you were Salma Hayek? How would your man react to seeing Cameron Diaz walk out of the kitchen? Now that you are plugged in, you are ready to turn it on.

Turn It On

As you make your entrance into the club, restaurant, or living room, catch the eye of as many people as possible. Don't seek it out; just pause, linger for a moment, and let their gaze be drawn to you. Remember, feeling confident and good about yourself is what makes you hot, and right now you are the hottest woman in the world. Of course they're going to notice you. Be careful here: You don't want an in-your-face, "I'm all that" quality, because that vibe makes you scary and unapproachable. Remember, men love strippers because they are *always* approachable. What you want here is a quiet awareness. You solved the Protein Folding Problem, and you are hyperconscious that now everyone wants a piece of you. Thoughts like "What? Oh, that's right . . . I forgot that I was the sexiest woman in the world for a minute. No wonder everyone is staring at me" should run through your head.

It takes a tremendous amount of energy to sustain this buzz for eight hours a night. The good news is that you need to do it only a couple of times a week. Remembering why you are so great will remind your man of why he thinks you're so great. He will notice the buzz around you and be drawn to your glow.

TEASE I: FLIRT

Dancers take all the energy they have worked up from exercises like these and pour it into two short sentences: "Hi, my name's Bambi. Would you like a dance?" It's always the same question, but every girl has her own time-tested approach. The most popular versions are:

- The Sex Kitten: These girls purr and hotly whisper, "Would you like a dance?" into to their customer's ear.
- The Big Easy: These girls lean over and show as much boob as possible without actually getting topless, before asking the key question.
- The Shiny Happy: These girls let their natural enthusiasm shine right on through, squealing, "Hi! Would! You! Like! A! Dance?!" to the surprised customer.
- The Benevolent Dictator: These girls command, "You. Dance," then proceed to take off their clothes while the hapless customer sits there, twenty-dollar bill clutched tightly in his palm, awestruck.

The approach is crucial, because it can shake up or soften whichever look a dancer has chosen for the night. For example, someone rocking the strong Intellectual or Personal Trainer look might choose a Sex Kitten approach to soften it up a bit. On the other hand, a Party Girl might try the Benevolent Dictator approach to show the customer that even though she's inebriated, she's still the boss.

Keeping a positive attitude is also important. As the adage goes, you have only one chance to make a first impression; so even when we're stressed, strippers never, ever act like "Oh, for God's sake, here are my tits, just give me the damned twenty dollars!" It does happen on occasion that a dancer completely loses it. She'll approach men in a pissed-off, cranky way, and of course she'll make no money and leave in tears. Men just don't respond to girls who are snobby, surly, angry, or unhappy. You've probably noticed that these approaches don't work very well at home with your man either. The truth is that most people respond best to suggestions or requests that are put to them in a certain way. I know from experience that the stripper approach is successful; after all, it's how I earn a living. Men respond best if they are approached in a way that leads them to believe that the stripper finds them the manliest, sexiest, most desirable man in the world. Men aren't there just to look at your knockers. Men want you to *want* to show them your knockers. They want to feel that you would like to dance for them. Not because of the twenty dollars in their pocket, but because you like to dance and, more importantly, you like them, as people, as men. Dancers in turn communicate this to their customers by flirting. Stripper flirting is pretty easy and can be broken down into four steps: a sexy, confident approach; eye contact; acting shy; and giggling.

Only you will know which approaches work best with your man. Try on one of the stripper styles just to see what happens. They will at the very least inject a sense of fun and play into your daily interactions. Here are some examples to try at home.

A.   The sexy approach

- The Sex Kitten: Purr and whisper into your man's ear, "Do you want chicken or spaghetti for supper?"
- The Big Easy: Unbutton your shirt, lean over, and press the sides of your boobs together with your arms. (*Caution: He won't actually be able to listen to anything while staring at your cleavage, so keep the conversation light.*)
- The Shiny Happy: "Yeah! I'd! Love! To! Watch! The! Game!"
- The Benevolent Dictator: "You. Sex. Let's go." And start taking off your clothes.

Any of these will surprise, amuse, and, depending on the topic, turn your man on, which is the whole point, after all.

The following three teases you probably already know, since they're likely how you got your man in the first place. But in case you need a refresher course, below are additional ways to let your man know you want him.

B.   Eye contact

Another great way to flirt is by using eye contact. This one's supereasy—all you need are eyes! Just stare at your man until he looks at you. When he catches you, quickly look away. It doesn't matter that you are thinking about the pot roast. It will look like you're having the same naughty thoughts you used to have when you first started dating him.

C.   Act Shy

It's hard to imagine that dancers act shy around their customers; after all, men don't come to strip clubs to meet shy women. They come for the inebriated bendy ones. But no matter what your strong points are as a stripper, acting shy is an important part of the flirt. All you have to do is blush a little, shrug a little, and be a little reluctant to talk about yourself. It doesn't matter that the customer has just seen you in a G-string, gyrating in front of him. Show a little modesty as he compliments the birthmark on your booty, and he'll be smitten.

D.   Giggle

Men love to make women laugh. They need to feel that they are witty and charming. Regardless of what we actually think, it's our job, as dancers, to reinforce their beliefs. Strippers go to great lengths to giggle like teenagers at a customer's joke, no matter how stupid or dirty. Obviously, we will draw the line at something bigoted or that we find personally offensive. Other than that, though, we can't get enough of their fart or one-legged blonde jokes. Now, like most women, you probably don't think many of your man's jokes are funny either. So try to find little things that you can giggle over. The giggle works so well because it is more than a laugh—it's a *flirty* laugh. It has a naughty, intimate feel to

it. The strategically placed giggle tells your man that not only is
he the wittiest man alive, but also the most desirable. P.S.: The
giggle works especially well if you touch his arm or, better yet,
thigh while you do it.

Tease 2: Girls Gone Wild!

In real life, men are taught to be the aggressors. And in a world
where men, as the pursuers, are often shut down by the "real"
women they approach at clubs and bars, it's nice for them to have
a place where a hot chick is not only happy to talk to them but
will show them her rack for a nominal fee. It's like a *Girls Gone
Wild* video where they get to be the host! Women don't usually
get this, but for men there is something tremendously likable
about a chick who will get naked for twenty bucks. It's just fun.
Even dancers who do the serious I'm-just-stripping-to-pay-for-
grad-school thing portray a fun, uninhibited quality that is miss-
ing in the women he works with or meets when he's out. It's a
quality that says, "Relax, this isn't serious—sex is fun." Case in
point: Many men think that Monica Lewinsky was *cool*. After all,
thong-flashing, frequent blow jobs, and creative use of cigars all
come pretty high up on a man's list of what he wants in a woman.

For men, an uninhibited woman is an easy woman, and men
love easy women. As someone once put it (okay, it was Pat
Benatar), love is a battlefield. Single men are soldiers who, after
meeting a woman, are prepared for a long and arduous struggle to
lay siege to her castle (i.e., get sex). Social custom dictates how
long the battle will last, usually between three and seven dates.
When a man does finally reach the castle, he finds that it is booby-
trapped (so to speak). Only by approaching and entering the castle

in a very specific way will he be able to finally conquer it. For the weary soldier, having lived through many such battles in his life, the easy woman is like the castle guardian who joyfully throws him the key to her kingdom and shouts, "Welcome!" as she hands him a nice cold brewski. Imagine a man's relief, then, when there is no battle or data analysis, just the promise of plain good ol' sex. Dancers are the embodiment of this wild, easy quality that men love.

Here's where it gets a little tricky, though. Dancers do like to drink and get naked, but we're actually not easy. I mean, sure, we'll take our dress off for twenty bucks, but in no way will you be getting anything resembling sex from us. Otherwise it wouldn't be a tease, and the customer wouldn't keep coming back for more. So here's how it works for you:

Get Naked

If it's been a while since a girl's done a dance, she'll jump up and say, "Oh my God! I love this song! I have to dance for you!" And she'll start peeling her dress off. What she's actually saying is, "Oh my God! I need to make some money! You're getting a dance whether you like it or not!" What the customer hears is, "Oh my God! This song makes me horny! And when I'm horny, I have to dance for you!"

Here's what you do at home: Wait until you and your man are alone together, and pop in a CD with a song on it that you really like. You can also do this with the radio or you can try a modified version in the car. When a song comes on that you love, jump up and exclaim, "Oh my God! I love this song!" and turn it up as loud as you like. Dance with all the abandon you've learned in the previous chapters' exercises. Involve your man as little or as much as you want. I actually did this at home to a bootlegged rap CD I bought off the street. My husband looked at me in shock until I backed my thang up, sat on his lap, and ground into him like a Vegas showgirl. When the next song came on, I said, "Oh, I don't really like this one," replaced it with the sports radio he had been listening to, and went about my business. The look of confusion and excitement on his face alone was worth it.

I Like My Liquor

If you drink, the next time you and your man are out, order something that will shock him. If you are strictly a white-wine-with-dinner kind of chick, order a shot of tequila. Or join him on the couch with a bottle of beer. It sounds silly, but if you throw in the odd "Whoo! I am so buzzed," it will bring your man back to his crazy college days with liberated coeds, when all you needed to do to score was ask.

The Power of Suggestion

Strippers are basically all talk and no action. We are not going to go home with a customer. What we are going to do is intrigue and entice him to go to the Champagne Room with us, at the rate of a tasty four hundred dollars an hour. How do we get a man to follow us anywhere? Simple. A couple of well-put sentences and we're gone in sixty seconds. A good line that always works is "Let's get out of here . . ." purred softly into his ear, à la the Sex Kitten. The customer usually just stands up and follows us to the Champagne Room like a meek little lamb. The second is saying something like "Can we go somewhere more private? I love talking to you, but I want to go somewhere more private so I concentrate on what you have to say." Again, this is said into his ear with the Sex Kitten purr, and a bit of the Big Easy body language thrown in. To try this yourself, wait till you and your man are out somewhere. When things start to get a little dull, seductively whisper, "Let's get out of here . . ." to him. If he doesn't stand up immediately, follow up with an "It's just so loud in here, I can hardly hear what you have to say, and I'd love to go somewhere more . . . you know . . . *private.*"

Then, instead of going home to bed, tease him by heading somewhere more intimate, like a dark café or a smoky dive bar, or even just sit in your car listening to soft jazz. While you're talking with him, no matter what it's about, pour on the flirt, especially the eye contact and the giggle. Knowing that he'll have to wait until he gets you home to play wrestler and ring girl with you will drive him crazy.

TEASE 3: TURN UP THE HEAT!

For a guy, there is no chance of a night at a strip club ending in sex (at least with us). It's actually this fact that makes dancing so sexy. When the customer isn't allowed to touch you, you are totally safe to be as hot as you want to be. Imagine that you're dancing for your man, George Clooney, or whoever you think is hot. Imagine pouring it on until you know the poor boy would give up a kidney just to be able to touch your thigh. Then, when you're through making him suffer, pat him on the bottom and send him off home to soothe himself with a bottle of hand cream and a few tissues. It sounds cruel, but it's not. Remember, the appeal of the strip club and the stripper is that guys want what they can't have. Your challenge, therefore, is to put up some of the boundaries at home that dancers have at the club. If you make it harder for your man to have you (in the biblical sense), he'll want you all the more.

A lot of self-help books actually advise something similar. When the spark goes out of your love life, experts suggest that you stop having sex and go back to doing things like holding hands, kissing, and groping instead. The idea is that when you're allowed to run only between bases one and three, you'll want to slide into home even more.

Personally, I think it's easier to find the naturally occurring boundaries in your daily life instead of erecting artificial ones. There are endless opportunities to tease your man: before you leave for work in the morning, during phone calls or instant messaging, before business trips or even jaunts to the grocery store. Here's the perfect example of how natural boundaries are effective: In a promo for an episode of the TV show *Everybody Loves Raymond*, Ray's wife soul-kisses him on her way out the door. He stands there for a beat, looking dumbfounded, then says shakily, "You can't kiss me like that! You activated the launch!" Your goal is to activate the launch sequence as often as you can when there's no opportunity for your man to act on it. Why? Again, men want what they can't have. Knowing that he won't be able to touch you again until much later that night will make him want you even more. Here are a few ways to turn up the heat, with varying degrees of flavor.

Mild

While you are getting dressed for work, let your man see you rolling up a pair of thigh-highs under your skirt or attaching them to your new garter belt.

Or while you are on the phone with him, say something innocent yet flirty, like "My neck is soooo stiff. I wish you were here to rub it." If you say it the right way, he'll wish he were there too.

Medium

Using the Sex Kitten voice, purr in his ear when you kiss him good-bye, "I can't wait till I get home to see you. What are you doing during lunch?" It doesn't matter that he has an important meeting planned. Just the possibility that you'd be up for a noon-time tryst will make him hot.

Spicy

Grab his package on your way out the door. Just go for it. If you've been building up to it by flirting more, he probably won't drop dead from shock. Then smile slyly and say, "See you later," as you walk away. Don't wait for him to follow—chances are he won't be able to walk for a while.

TEASE 4: NO SEX IN THE CHAMPAGNE ROOM

A few years ago, the song "Everybody's Free to Wear Sunscreen" came out. It was actually a graduation commencement speech, rumored to have been written by Kurt Vonnegut, set to music. (In fact it was written by Mary Schmich.) It offered sage bits of wisdom such as "Do one thing every day that scares you" and, of course, "Wear sunscreen." A couple of months later, comedian Chris Rock put together his own version, also chock-full of timely advice, including "No matter what a stripper tells you, there is no sex in the Champagne Room." And he's right; there's not. Most of the time, we just sit around and talk. So what do men pay four hundred dollars an hour to sit around and talk about? Sex, of course.

Can I Get Fries with That?

What men want the most is to hear all about what you like. As women, you can't (and apparently don't) talk about sex enough. Anything you want to tell them about your body and what makes it tick is welcome, from how you hate having your hair pulled during sex to how your ears tingle when you are really turned on. Fantasies, favorite positions—all of it. Men have inquiring minds, and they want to know.

Tread Carefully!

The thing men *hate* the most is having a serious conversation about . . . well . . . anything. Sex talk with your partner should always be fun and flirty. Otherwise, your man will jump on the defensive and tune you out. This makes sense, in a way. Having a serious sex talk means that you're dissatisfied—and as far as they're concerned there are only two possible reasons for that: 1) they, as men, are total, incompetent losers or 2) you're too demanding. Either way, you end up frustrated, with your man confused and unhappy.

Madonna? Whore?

Another reason you have to be careful is that men have that whole virgin/slut thing. Even if you're a stripper, guys don't want to know that you've danced for ten years or have slept with twenty-five people. Guys all want the stripper who's been dancing for under a year, who's doing it to pay for college, and who, depending on her age, has had sex with a maximum of five partners. So if you've been with your guy for a long time, you don't want to toss him a clue by saying, "I always love it when guys grab my hooters really hard." Instead of getting the hint, he'll just be thinking, Which guys? When? How many?

I Said, Turn Left

Likewise, when it's put the wrong way, telling your man what you want can sound like criticism. A more general "I love finishing first because then I can concentrate on you" is always better than "I wish you would let me go first for once!" or, worse, "No, not there! Back up! No! Where you were before, bonehead!"

2 + 1 = Threesome!

Every guy I have ever met has had the fantasy of being with two girls at once. At least a couple of times a night a guy will have me dance for or with another stripper. In addition, a lot of times a man will bring his wife or girlfriend into the club, with the unspoken hope that he can get her into the fantasy too.

As a rule, the threesome always comes up in Champagne Room talk. When a guy inevitably asks me if I've ever played for the home team, I always reply, "No, but it's on my list of things to do." Which is true. I'll tell them that I've never met anyone I'd want to get busy with, but if Britney Spears asked me nicely, I'd probably say yes. What usually follows is a fun comparison of our celebrity wish lists—women (and men) who we'd like to have cook our eggs in the morning.

How to Grant Their Wish in Fantasy

You can try this at home, just by saying something like "Damn! Christina Aguilera is smokin'!" And watch as confusion and desire war for control of your man's face while images of the three of you rolling around in bed float through his mind.

If you and your man have never talked about other women, or if you are totally grossed out by the idea of being with another woman, that's fine too. Just tell your man specifically why, and he'll go nuts. "Yes, Halle Berry is hot, but I like dick, and this is why . . ." Actually, guys would rather hear you say this than have you drop in the odd "Janet's abs are *so* tight" every now and then. However, if you are so inclined, be as graphic as you want to be. The best real-life sex I ever had was when my husband asked me for details of what I would do with the other (fantasy) woman if she were there. As I told him, we both got totally hot and had amazing sex.

TEASE 5: THE DANCE

Doing a dance for your man might feel a little forced or weird if it comes out of nowhere. It's best to gradually lead up to it by doing some of the other teases first. That way, when you sit him down and tell him not to move because you've got a little something to show him, he'll have some idea of what to expect. Below you'll find complete instructions on how to give a classic New York City lap dance. In a way, this type of lap dance perfectly reflects the city it comes from: It's got cutting-edge style and fantastic presentation. The one drawback is that you won't get a whole lot of bang for your buck; the New York–style lap dance is all about the tease. There's strictly no touching allowed, so you will have (depending on the songs you choose) at least eight or nine blissful minutes where you can make your man suffer mercilessly by teasing him with your luscious self and he won't be able to do anything about it. If you're looking for a more "hands on" experience when you do your dance, check out the alternate endings at the end of this chapter. They'll give you some ideas on how to get you and your man a grand finale.

Setting the Stage

Dancing for your partner takes careful planning. The first thing you want to decide is what you are going to wear. From chapter 4, "Stripper Chic," you've learned what you like, what looks good on you, how to move in it, and, more importantly, how to get it off without tripping. So choose something that you feel confident wearing and have done at least a few practice dances in. Personally, I love stripping out of lingerie like bras, garters, and hose. For the home theater, I would definitely recommend the following: high heels, thigh-high hose, a G-string, and a matching lacy push-up bra. Choose a color you feel confident in. Black, white, and red are standard, but shops like Victoria's Secret also offer a huge selection of matching lingerie sets in great colors like coral and turquoise.

Over the Top

As I mentioned, strippers in New York wear long or short dresses over their G-strings, and the dress is what comes off during the dance. During Halloween and Christmas, some clubs have their dancers dress up in costumes or Santa outfits. As silly as it might sound, I feel a million times sexier dancing in a devil outfit than I do in a spandex dress. It makes the show more silly and fun, which customers really enjoy. Whatever you choose to wear over your ensemble should make you feel as sexy and confident as the lingerie itself does. Furthermore, it should also be easy to dance in and easy to take off. Simple tube or halter dresses are good choices. You can even costume it up if you'd like. There's no need to go out and buy something special—some of the stuff you have lying around your closet can make great fantasywear. For example, grab a pair of short shorts, a denim shirt, and a cowboy hat for an urban cowgirl look. I also know from experience that most men will go nuts if you strip out of one of their suit jackets and a tie. Remember Kim Basinger in *9½ Weeks*? Throw one of his work shirts over your lingerie, and he'll never wash it again.

The Set

At my club, dancers do three-song sets onstage. The first song is danced with the dress on, the second song with just the top of the dress down, and the third and final song is with the dress completely off. For dancing at home, this is a good routine to follow. It gives you an entire song with your clothes on to get into the mood and feel comfortable, and it gives your man some time to pick his jaw up off the floor.

TIMING

Each of the three songs should be about, or just under, three minutes. Too short and you don't have enough time to bust out all of your moves; too long and you run out of moves altogether.

Music

You will need to burn a CD or make a tape of the songs you want to dance to. It's a no-brainer that it's easier to dance slowly to slow, sexy music. Some stripper faves are Enigma's "Sadeness" and anything by the singer Sade—but it really is all about what you like. Personally, I prefer the soothing sounds of a dental drill to a Sade CD, but that's just me. I'm a punker at heart, so I like dancing to fast, fun music like the Ramones, Sex Pistols, or Blink 182. I still dance slowly, though. After all, I am wearing five-inch heels, and *no one* looks good moshing naked.

For me, the music will make or break a stage set. When I am totally into the songs, I lose myself and become part rock star, part video vamp, and part sex goddess. It's important that the music you choose, no matter what it is, makes you feel the same way.

THE ORDER

The order of the songs is important too. When I'm onstage, I prefer to have the last song be the strongest. The first two songs I'll pick will be feel-good favorites like AC/DC's "You Shook Me All Night Long" or Ozzy Osbourne's "Crazy Train." The last song will be something that everyone loves but that they haven't heard in forever, like Def Leppard's "Rock of Ages" or the Scorpions' "Rock You Like a Hurricane." When one of these songs comes on, you automatically feel the energy in the club change. My goal when I dance onstage is to pump everyone up so that they feel good. I know that when my set is over, all of those men will want to buy a dance from me. For you, the last song you dance to can either energize your man or cool him down—it's entirely up to you, and what you plan on doing after the show is over. More than likely, when the set ends you'll be having crazy monkey sex, so make sure the rest of the CD is music you won't feel weird booming to.

Seating

You'll need to find a chair for your man to sit in while you do the dance. Optimally, it should be a low chair with a medium-high back and padded armrests. No, wait . . . there is a reason. It's easier to lean in toward a man who is lower, and some of the moves will require something to rest your head and knees on. A kitchen chair with arms is best, but a La-Z-Boy recliner, captain's chair, or couch will do just fine.

Atmosphere

Set up the chair in the room you'll be doing the dance in. Make sure you have plenty of room to move, that it's warm and comfortable, and that your neighbors can't see in. Set up the CD player so that all you have to do is hit the play button and go.

Lighting

A strip club's lighting is hard to re-create for the home theater, what with the disco ball and strobe lights and all. Candles are a good choice because their light is soft, dim, and flattering. You can also use scented candles if you want—just don't gas your man out with anything too heavy or girly. Single-note florals like gardenia or honeysuckle are good. Some perfume companies also make candles, so if you're an Opium addict (the perfume, not the drug) you can fill the room (and his imagination) with your signature scent.

If candles aren't an option, throw a fifteen-watt bulb in a table lamp. Then put a sheer scarf or two over it to dim the lighting to a comfortable level. Don't use synthetic fabrics, or they might catch on fire. In fact, throwing anything over a lit bulb is a hazard, so use extreme caution. You want the showstopper to be taking your dress off, not calling the fire department. If you don't have any scarves (I don't), you can use a cotton oxford or something like it. Use warm colors—yellow, pink, or bronzes; they're more flattering on your skin than cool shades like blue or green.

Timing

Pick a time when you won't be interrupted and when the music and/or noises you might make won't interrupt anyone else. Probably the best time to try this is after you've both been out for an intimate dinner or cocktail. Your hair and makeup will already be done, so all you have to do when you get home is tell your man to sit like a good boy and not beg.

Go for It!

Dim the lights to a level where you feel comfortable, turn on the music, and go for it. Remind your partner that he's not allowed to touch you; if he tries, firmly but politely remove his hands. This will drive him nuts. In a good way.

SONG 1

1. Enter the room and pause. Let him just look at how hot you are.
2. Move forward and position yourself between the knees of your partner.
3. Hike up the front of your dress, high enough to expose your G-string. Hang out there long enough to let him think about what's underneath it.
4. Make eye contact with your partner and hold his stare. If you feel too silly or self-conscious, one stripper trick is to lean in and bring your face really close to his. Basically, you want to put your lips about an inch away from your partner's lips. Instead of staring him in the eye, gaze down at his mouth instead. To him, it will look like you are close enough to kiss.
5. Since you are already leaning in toward him, stand up slightly and rest your hands on the back of his chair, so that his face is about an inch away from your cleavage. Then let go of the chair and squeeze your breasts together with your hands. Let him get a good close-up view of how totally hot they are—whatever their size.
6. Stand back, about a foot or so away from him, and

dance to the music. *You should be about halfway through the first song.*

7. Turn your back to him and bend your knees as though you were about to sit on his lap.

8. Roll your booty up and down (the way girls in music videos do).

9. If you feel comfortable, bend over and lift the back of your dress, giving him a full-on view of your G-string-clad butt. Don't worry—all butts, big *and* small, look sexy in this position.

10. Reach between your legs and stroke your inner thigh.

11. Stand up and turn to the side. Lean in toward him, resting your arm on the back of his chair. Stay low (your knees will be slightly bent), so that your boobs are at his eye level. *This should be the end of song 1.*

SONG 2

1. Leaning in and staying low, slowly peel the top of your dress down. If you are wearing a bra, remove whatever you have chosen to wear over it completely, so that you will do your second dance in just your lingerie. The rest of the steps will work whether you are topless now or not.

2. Keep your boobs a few inches from his face and slowly run your free hand over them.

3. Stand up and face your man.

4. Lean in toward him, placing your hands on the back of the chair, one hand on either side of his head. Keep your boobs as close to his face as you can, and remember to move in time with the music.

5. Next, move so that both your arms are to one side of his head, and place your hands on the back of the chair. Lean in as far as you can, resting your weight on the back of the chair. Get as close to your man as you can without actually touching him (or touch him, if that's part of the plan) so that, looking down, he sees only your back and butt.

6. Move back from him slightly, keeping your hands on the back of the chair. If you are leaning to his right, put your left knee up on the left armrest. You will be in a sort of straddle position over his lap. Free your left arm and use it to caress yourself, wherever you want. Keep your right arm on the chair back for support. Again, remember to move with the music and keep the flow. *At this point, you should be about halfway through the second song.*

7. Stand up and turn your back toward him again.

8. If you are bendy, lean backward, as if you are going into a backbend position, until your head rests either on the back of the chair or on his shoulder. The lower the chair back, the more difficult this is, so try to pick a chair that has a relatively high back. Once you're in this position, your man should be staring directly down at your breasts. If you aren't bendy, do a few booty rolls, then stand up and slide onto your knees on the floor in front of him. If you aren't bendy but are making this a contact dance, just sit on his lap and rest your head on his shoulder. Then just move on to step 10 and proceed.

9. Hang out here for as long as you can.

10. Press your boobs together with your hands, and feel free to touch and caress yourself as much as you want.

11. Slide down your man, onto your knees.

12. Rest the back of your head on his inner thigh and caress your face, all the while looking up at him. *You should now be ending your second song.*

SONG 3

This is basically a repeat of song 2, with slightly more emphasis on your butt.

1. Stand up slowly, dancing all the while with the music, and remove the rest of your dress, or your bra if you are now down to lingerie.

2. Kick the dress out of your way so you don't trip, or pick it up and throw it on top of your partner's head or wherever it will make him look silliest.

3. Okay. Now lean in low, with your hands on the back of the chair, one on each side of his head.

4. When you have your balance, release one arm and slowly run your free hand over your naked boobs. Move in time with the music.

5. Next, put both arms on the back of his chair, either to the left or to the right of his head. Lean in as far as you can, so that, again, looking down, he sees only your butt upturned in his lap.

6. Roll your booty in time with the music.

7. Slowly stand and turn around so that your back is to him.

8. Lean forward and bend over, as if you were doing a yoga stretch or trying to touch your toes.

9. Stay here for a few seconds to allow him to take in the view.

10. Come to a partial stand, as if you were going to sit on his lap.

11. Do a few more booty rolls. Keep looking over your shoulder at him while you do this. It will remind him of how much fun doggie-style is.

12. Turn around to face your man, and then just dance until the song is over. If you are bendy or have any special moves I haven't mentioned, now's the time to bust them out—it is the grand finale, after all. Finally, when the third song is over, remove your G-string and

13. Have fierce sex.

Whatever you do, don't use any of these moves in a real strip club unless 1) a client hits you with a million dollars in cash up front (hey, everybody has their price) or 2) you are dancing for the lead singer of Sugar Ray.

STRIPPER TIPS!

The most important thing about dancing for your man is that you enjoy yourself. Here are a couple of tips that will help:

- Know every single beat of every single song as well as you know your own name. Strippers dance to the same songs onstage, at least a couple of times a night, four or five nights a week. The better you know the songs you choose, the easier it will be to feel comfortable dancing to them. You'll also be able to tweak the choreography to fit the song. Build up your man's anticipation by waiting until the shotgun-blast chorus of Bon Jovi's "It's My Life" to take your top down or dress off.

- Strippers give a couple of hundred dances *a week*. The least you can do is practice once or twice.
- Keep the focus on you—not your man. Remember in chapter 1 when I said that the only three things a dancer thinks about while giving a dance are getting the customer into the VIP room, how much money she's made, and whether she's shown the customer her butt? The point is that dancers are not worried about whether the customer likes her or thinks she looks okay. You shouldn't be either. Don't dance for your man because you want him to think you're sexy or to turn him on. Dance for your man *only* if it's something that makes you feel sexy and turns you on.

There you have it: a typical New York lap dance. Still, variety is the spice of life, and there's a big, wonderful world of lap-dance styles out there to choose from.

Around the World in Eighty Dances

Okay, it's really four. As you've learned, the rules about what you are and aren't allowed to do during a dance vary from club to club and city to city. If you've already danced for your man and want to try something new, or if you found the above description on how to give a dance too tame, here are some variations that are sure to add the spice you need. They've been inspired by cities and countries around the world.

THE FLORIDA

Florida is famous for their spectacular nude clubs, where tanned hotties will take it all off for a tip. So this one's easy. Just do everything listed in the above dance, only do it naked. For this you'll need a special G-string. There are two kinds. The first is called a "breakaway" because its sides include a button or snap for easy on/off capability. The second is a simple string thong whose sides are tied together in cute little bows, à la the string bikini. (Or you could just use . . . a string bikini.) During the third song, right after step 2, in addition to removing your bra simply remove your G-string as well. Then finish the dance as directed in all your buck-naked God-given glory. Have sex, repeat.

THE LAS VEGAS

You know how I told you to forget everything you learned from watching the movie *Showgirls*? (I mean, apart from the fact that Elizabeth Berkley can't act. Sorry—that was just too easy.) When it comes to Las Vegas, the movie is actually pretty realistic. That's why Vegas girls are famous for putting the *lap* in the *lap dance.* Anyone who's had a dance anywhere else after trying out Vegas knows that they are getting a pale imitation of the VIP treatment they can get at any L.V. club. Rules vary from club to club, so you can do this dance one of two ways.

1. This is a variation of steps 7 through 10 of the first song. Keep step 7 as is: Turn your back to him and bend your knees as though you were about to sit on his lap. Then instead of step 8, where you'd roll your booty up and down the way girls in music videos do, actually sit down on his lap. At this point he should have at least popped a semi. If not, you'll still have a pretty

good idea of how it's hanging. Once you've figured it out, grind your butt into his manhood a few times. (Be careful here: A little friction goes a long way! You don't want to pull, pinch, or abrade anything.) This is guaranteed to bring a softy or semi into a full-fledged, raging hard-on. After you know you've gotten to him (he may groan, whimper, or beg for mercy) stand up and continue with steps 9 and 10. Repeat these alternate steps during song 2 (after you've taken your top down). Instead of just showing him your booty, show him what you can do with your booty and grind into him some more. Finally, during song 3, after you've taken everything off except your G-string, you have a choice of either grinding into him instead of doing dance steps 7 through 11 or grinding into him until his very end.

2. Las Vegas clubs are notorious for their lax "no touching" rule. It's what the customers bank on when they go to an L.V. club. If you want to be in total control of your man and the situation, do the L.V. dance above but stick to the New York rules. If you want to bring a little *authenticity* to the dance, then tell your man it's okay to touch you—and tell him where. Although touching is permitted in Vegas, the exchange of bodily fluids is not, and that should be your guide in telling your man where he can put his hands. The only caution for this dance is about the setup. If you are going to be grinding into him and you're going to be letting him run his man hands all over your body, don't

do it in the bedroom! Set up the dance in the living
room, kitchen, hallway, whatever. If you do the L.V.
dance in the privacy of your bedroom, it's likely to lead
to sex before you even get a chance to take anything
off—not that that's bad.

THE LOS ANGELES

If you really want to show your man what a superstar you are,
change the lighting setup. Grap a clip-on table light with a mov-
able head, or a simple portable floodlight. Pop in the highest-watt
bulb you can find—probably a 150. Keeping the rest of the room
pitch-black, aim the lamp, spotlight-style, at the area where you'll
be dancing. This is a great setup because spotlights are flattering;
they're so bright they just wash out any of your flaws. (Think of
Nicole Kidman dancing in the car headlights to "Sweet Home
Alabama" in the movie *To Die For*.) Another plus about the light
being so bright is that you won't be able to see your man or his
reaction, and thus you'll be able to concentrate on the dance and
tune him out—until the point where he grabs you and throws you
over his shoulder, that is.

THE BANGKOK

If you're bendy and not at all shy about it, this is the dance for
you. For the Bangkok, keep song 1 exactly the same. Then get
naked at the beginning of song 2. And instead of actually dancing,
just bust out the props you've brought along (a vibrator, whip, set
of Ping-Pong balls, whatever) and get busy. Men love to watch
women, and men especially love to watch women love themselves, if you know what I mean. The only caution here is that you

might want to tie your man securely to his chair; otherwise, like an overeager Michael Bolton fan, he'll jump up onstage to become a part of your show.

If you do think you'd like to make props part of your show, here are some things to consider:

- Vibrators. Men intimidate easily, so choose the vibrator that least resembles an actual penis. I remember the first time I showed my husband my Rabbit vibrator—which has a 6-inch shaft, 1½-inch diameter, and provides nonstop clitoral stimulation via a built-in rabbit-shaped device that sits on the front of the shaft. He was so put off by it that he wouldn't have sex with me for a week.

- Whips and chains. If this is something you and your man have discussed but never tried, start off slowly. Do not begin your dance by bringing out the bullwhip. Tie him up gently with silken scarves, and nip at him softly with long, plumed feathers, a soft leather switch, or even pliable wood, like a willow switch. Flirtcatalog.com has a great link to fetish clothes and props, which will give you a good idea on where to get started.

- Your best friend. Obviously, the best accessory for a totally hot lap dance is your bi-curious sorority sister. Still, even if you and your man have talked about a threesome, make sure he knows what you've got planned. Some things that seem great in fantasy are really just freaky and weird in real life.

After you've done the checking and gotten the go-ahead, keep in mind that timing is everything. As with the basic lap dance, you want to build your man's anticipation song by song. So save up your props (or use them sparingly) until the very last song. For example, if you brought a vibrator, bring it out and turn it on for a second or two a couple of times during the first two songs. Toy with it by touching yourself quickly, then putting it away while you continue to dance. Wait until the last song before putting "El Matador" to work. Similarly, you'll want to start off slowly with whatever tools you choose. As I mentioned in the "Stripper Tips" section, it'll definitely help you feel more comfortable if you get a few practice runs in before the big game.

So there you have it: a step-by-step guide to what dancers do to captivate a man. Now that you too have the power to bring any man to his knees, use it carefully and wisely. And always, *always* use your power for good instead of evil.

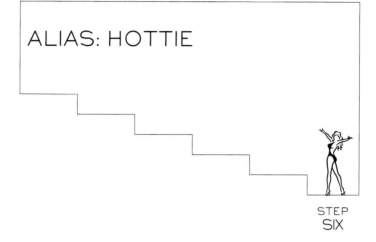

ALIAS: HOTTIE

STEP
SIX

By following the steps in this book, you, like a CIA agent superspy, have learned 1) a repertoire of moves especially designed to bring men to their knees and 2) how to use interesting gadgets and devices (okay, they're really sex toys, but whatever). The final step in unleashing your inner hottie is to choose a name for her. You have earned it, Grasshopper.

Every stripper has a stage name she dances by. A dancer's name has several purposes. First, it offers a modicum of protection against potential stalkers. I've never actually heard of any, but it's always good to play it safe. Second, it keeps us focused and professional. When someone calls you by your code name, you know you are on the job with a mission to accomplish. The third and most important purpose of having a stage name is that it allows us to do some creative role-playing.

ON A ROLE

By now you know that all strippers are not twenty-three-year-old girls who dance for the sheer fun of it. But a thirty-five-year-old dancer with a husband and two grade-school kids might want customers to think that's who she is. So in addition to rocking the Party Girl persona, she'll also choose a name that reflects who she wants the audience to believe she is. For example, a dancer might choose a clean, preppy-sounding name like Carolyn, Haley, or Michelle. These tell the customer that she is young, comes from a good home, and is probably stripping to pay her undergrad tuition. Some dancers choose sporty, bi-gender names like Jordan, Taylor, or Dylan. These tell customers that she is fun, listens to loud music, and is both politically and sexually liberal. Other dancers like more exotic names, such as Giselle, Margherita, or Adrianna. Names like these tell the customer that she is passionate, spicy, and can party you under the table.

Some names, like those listed above, naturally lend themselves to certain ideas or images. For example, the name Kate always sounds clean-cut, while Brandi always sounds slutty. In addition, some dancer names work because they cause the customer to make certain mental connections. A stripper using the stage name Pamela or Britney can't help conjuring up comparisons to Pamela Anderson or Britney Spears.

GLOSSARY

Here is a list of the top twenty-five stripper names, with their meanings attached:

ALEXIS: The ultimate bitchy name. Works best on pouty brunettes with small breasts and big attitudes.

ASHLEY: Dirty South. Ashleys have soft hair, soft voices, and howl like monkeys during sex.

AMBER: A soft, sexy name for girls that are one or two IQ points shy of Mensa.

BAILEY: Named after a brand of liquor. Enough said.

BRITTANY OR BRITNEY: Thanks to Ms. Spears, there's actually a waiting list for strippers who want to use this name.

CHRISTI: Superfriendly! Works best on former cheerleaders and future porn stars.

CHANTAL: The first choice for upwardly mobile aging blondes and second wives everywhere.

CINDY: Superfriendly but young. Best for girls whose older sisters are cheerleaders or porn stars.

DYLAN: Good for tough, artsy, ambi-sexual girls.

HEATHER: The ultimate popular-girl name. There's a waiting list for this one too.

JAIME: Different, smart, artsy. A good California Girl name.

JASMINE: A soft, pretty name that works with any look or ethnicity.

JENNIFER OR JENNY: Heather's best friend.

JESSICA: Jennifer's friend who also wants to be friends with Heather but isn't.

JORDAN: A sultry name that works for any ethnic background.

KATE OR KATIE: Preppy, cute. A good choice for a Meg Ryan look-alike (I think she's played someone named Kate in at least ten of her movies).

MADISON: Snooty, sexy. Just like Paris Hilton.

MICHELLE: Earnest, all-American.

MELISSA: A girly, pretty name for a girly, pretty girl.

RYAN: Jaunty, sexy, tomboy.

SIENNA OR SIERRA: Earthy, cowgirl-cool.

TIFFANY: Uptown girl.

TAYLOR: Ivy League liberal, smart.

TYLER: Only if Taylor is taken.
XENA: Funny, strong.

As you can see, a dancer's stage name generally corresponds with her persona or look, which we explored back in chapter 4. Here's how we connect the dots:

STRIPPER LOOK	NAME
The Bombshell	Britney, Pamela, Naomi
The Video Vixen	Alexis, Jackson, Jameson
The Party Girl	Amber, Christi, Cindi, Nicki, Dawn
The Exotic	Paola, Arianna, Valentina, Sophia
The California Girl	Jaime, Summer, Meadow, Willow
The Uptown Girl	Ashley, Chantal, Jillian, Madison
The Intellectual	Dylan, Veruka, Niko
The Personal Trainer	Shauna, Chyna, Xena

Hi, My Name Is . . .

When I first started dancing, I used my real name, Jessica, as my stage name. It wasn't for lack of imagination—rather, it was too much imagination that burdened me. I couldn't pin down which name I wanted. I worshipped Marilyn, but it was too old-fashioned. I wanted something pink and soft-sounding—something that evoked beauty, innocence, and a certain untouchable quality. Summer was taken, Fawn was too soon after the Iran-

Contra scandal (for you youngsters, it's Oliver North's secretary Fawn Hall whom I'm referring to), and Bambi just sounded like a hooker. Finally, foraging into my black hole–like memory of useless pop-culture information, I lighted on the embodiment of who I wanted to represent: a blonde built like a brick house, and certainly on an intellectual par with one: Melody, the bodacious drummer from Josie and the Pussycats.

The name Melody suited me well when I started dancing at twenty-three. Somehow it perfectly captured the age and level of sexual maturity (i.e., not very) where I was at the time. As I grew older, though, Melody no longer fit. Which isn't to say I didn't use it: I did. I worked it like a bad Vegas lounge lizard until the dark day when I accompanied my then boyfriend to his boss's wedding. As Ryan and I were making the rounds, he spotted his best friend (whom I'd never met) and excitedly said, "Oh, there's Pete! Pete! Over here!" Pete and his girlfriend, Kiki, warmly greeted us, and I smiled and shook their hands and said, "Hi, I'm Melody." Suddenly, there was a dead silence as Pete and Kiki stopped smiling and looked at each other in confusion. Now, both of them knew that my name was Jessica—Ryan had already told them about me, months before. Because they knew that my name was Jessica, they also knew that my name was *not* Melody. Further, they were both perfectly aware that the name Jessica didn't even resemble the name Melody. Jessica, Melody. Different opening sounds; different closing sounds . . . You get the picture.

I suppose it would have been somewhat plausible for me to have accidentally called myself Jennifer or even Jasmine if by that point I'd had a bit to drink, but I had not. Instead, I'd very soberly announced my name to be something very different-sounding from my own: *"Melody."*

It hung out there, heavy and oppressive, for a full minute or two as I imagined the sound of crickets coming through the walls and drowning out the orchestra.

I'm pretty sure I was sputtering too. "I'm sorry," I said, looking at Kiki. "I don't think I caught that. Did you say your name was Melody?"

"No," she said, looking at me, in confusion. "It's . . . Kiki."

"Oh, okay . . . I don't know where I got that from," I said. "I think I was distracted for a minute. Sorry." Then Ryan jumped in and the moment passed. Of course, to this day, Pete and Kiki still think I'm daft.

After that incident, I began changing my dance name every few months, whenever I started feeling a little too comfortable or as my look or attitude changed. As Melody, I had short, platinum-blond hair. After I got long, dark brown hair extensions, it no longer fit. With dark hair I felt sexy, powerful, rebellious, and a little pissed off. I chose to dance by the name Petra and pretended to have an Australian accent. A few months later, after the anger had subsided and the hair extensions were out, a name I had always liked opened up: Kayla. Kayla nicely summed up everything I wanted to convey to the customer. It had the clean, preppy sound of the hard *K,* which suited where I was from (Martha's Vineyard) and my (sort of) educated personality. But the name itself was exotic, which fit my look: Portuguese, Polish, English, and Irish. Kayla suited me so well that I decided to stick with it. Sadly, I still have to stop for a minute and concentrate when strangers I meet ask my name, but it's been well worth it.

As you can see, role-playing is a helpful way for dancers to find their stripper names. For me, it took three tries. As Melody, I played the Party Girl, and as Petra I played the Intellectual. But Kayla gives me the freedom to go between Video Vixen, Intellectual, and Exotic, without losing the key qualities that make me who I am. At home, you can try the following exercise for preparation.

EXERCISE: I'M NOT A…

Sometimes it's easier to define yourself by who you're *not* than by who you are. Finding things that you're sure you don't like can often be easier than finding things you do.

To begin: Go over the detailed list of stripper looks in chapter 4 and find one or two that you like. These would be the looks and attitude you think you might have if you were an actual stripper. For example, you might feel a particular affinity with the Uptown Girl or the California Girl.

Now find the one or two that you are most strongly opposed to. For example, you might feel particularly horrified at the thought of working at a strip club as a Party Girl or a Video Vixen. My personal polar opposite is the Personal Trainer. After all, there's a reason why I know how to apply different shades of tanner to fake the look of toned muscles—I have no muscle tone of my own to speak of.

Once you have found the stripper that you are least likely to be . . . do a dance as her. There's no need to get dressed up or anything. Just turn on the radio and dance to any old song. Imagine there is some random customer sitting in the kitchen chair, and do a dance for him the way you think that your opposite would. You might find that this is a little difficult at first. If you happen to be born with a more serious temperament, for instance, you might have a hard time getting into the spirit of the Party Girl.

Ask yourself these questions to get into the mood: How would you approach a customer for a dance? What topics of conversation would you bring up? How would you move when you actually give the dance? Then just do it. Don't hold back—and have fun! When the song is over, sit down and think about what ideas or feelings occurred to you while you were dancing. Maybe you'll come up with a confirmation of why you could never, ever be a Party Girl, or maybe you'll come up with new thoughts and ideas on what kind of dancer you definitely would be.

As you can see from the above exercise, role-playing is fun, and it's good for you too. It's well known that make-believe is an important part of a child's development. And, as it turns out, make-believe is every bit as good for grown-ups as it is for kids. An important research article in the *Journal of Personality and Social Psychology* (December 2002) concluded that college students who acted outgoing and happy actually *became* more outgoing and happy. In three separate studies, college students in different situations were asked to act extroverted and record their moods and feelings. In two short-term experiments and one long-term study, students who behaved in an outgoing manner generally reported elevated moods and happier feelings, while most students who were asked to behave in an introverted and shy manner reported feelings of dissatisfaction and unhappiness.

The research suggests that we have more power over our emotions and outlook than we may think we do. It also gives credence to the popular self-help idea that our subconscious thoughts and beliefs are an instrumental part of what creates our reality.

If acting happy can make you happy, it makes sense to conclude that acting sexy can make you sexy. And actually, this is true. Like I said at the beginning, dancers are *made,* not born. We come to the club with the same fears and issues that anyone else has. It's only learning by imitation and approximation that we ourselves become this sexy. Throughout this book you've done many exercises to get you in touch with your own sexuality. By replicating the steps dancers take to truly own their sexuality, you have started on the process to truly owning yours. You now feel comfortable with your naked self, and when your ego's especially down, you know what to do to pick it back up. You know how to look, dress, and act sexy. You even know how to dance sexy. So it's time to put the package together by finding a name.

GETTING STARTED

In the beginning of your shamanic quest to find the name of your inner hottie, it works well to use the names of others you admire. For example, if it's too difficult to dance around your living room naked as plain old you, then do it pretending that you are Britney Spears. You will find that it gets amazingly easy. Use whatever images inspire you. You know as well as I do that there is some celebrity out there, right this very minute, that you would love to be—whether just for a minute or just for a day, going to the grocery store or going out on an important date. It doesn't matter who, or what the reason is. It could be Janet Jackson or Janet Reno, Sandra Bullock or Sandra Day O'Connor. Whatever quality it is about someone that you love and admire is between you and you alone. Embrace it completely, then try the basic striptease, all the while imagining that you're lifting up your judicial robes instead of a spandex dress.

Tradition!

Formulas vary, but the traditional way to find your stripper name is to add your middle name to the name of the first street you lived on. So if your name is Tammy Faye Bakker and you grew up on Scary Lane, your stripper name would be Faye Scary. Obviously, this is not how real strippers arrive at their stage names, but it's fun to try.

Porn Star Name

Just so you know, there's also a method to come up with your porn star name. Take the name of your first pet and add it to your current street address. So if your first pet was named Tiger and you now live on Woods Street, your porn star name would be Tiger Woods. Oh, wait . . .

When we were living in New York City, my porn star name was Cookie Front, and my husband's was Spanky Front. How great was that? It's fun to have a porn star name, just for the laugh factor—even if you don't plan on watching or making one.

Drag Queen Name

If you're feeling really crazy, another fun name to have is a drag queen name. Drag queens are all about the drama, so it's good to have a drag queen name when you are feeling so fabulous that you just can't contain it, or you find that you have actually turned into Auntie Mame. For a drag queen name, you need to be very creative and heavy on the puns. For example, a friend of mine dubbed her then country-music-loving, fanatical right-wing fiancé

Miss Reba Publican. Another friend, dolled up in a naughty-nursie uniform for Halloween, dubbed herself—to the horror of all—Miss Kitty Catheter.

You get the idea here. Find a word (or two) that best sums you up and split it up or twist it around until you can get at least a couple of meanings out of it. Then throw a "Miss" in front, and you're good to go. For example, the word that best suits me is *chaos,* because things always seem to break in my presence. I'm also a huge fan of author Patricia Cornwell's lead character, Kay Scarpetta. For these reasons, my drag queen name is Miss Kay Oss.

The important point here is to play around and have fun with it. You can even try an anagram—just scramble the letters in your first and last names and see what new names, words, or phrases come up. If you're open to it, inspiration can be found anywhere.

SOURCES FOR INSPIRATION

Movies

It's hard to find great movies with strong female leads whose names are worth mentioning. Fortunately, there are plenty of mediocre movies out there to choose from. Here are a few where the hot chicks also kick ass! *The Long Kiss Goodnight, Charlie's Angels* (1 and 2), *Speed, Double Jeopardy, Tomb Raider* (1 and 2), *Alien, Aliens, Terminator 2, The Matrix* trilogy, and, of course, *Kill Bill* (Volumes 1 and 2).

TV

You'll definitely find more strong, sexy *real* women on TV than you will in the theater. Here are some to check out, sorted by genre: Reality: *Survivor.* It's the only game in town. Drama: *Buffy the Vampire Slayer, Sex and the City, Alias, CSI, CSI Miami, Dead Like Me, Gilmore Girls, Law & Order* (all three versions), *Six Feet Under,* and *Without a Trace.* Comedy: *Friends, Scrubs, Will and Grace.*

Music

Ani DiFranco, Liz Phair, Lucinda Williams, Beth Orton, Joan Jett, the Dixie Chicks, Sheryl Crow, Gwen Stefani, Dido, Tori Amos, Sarah McLachlan. You will never hear one of these rocker chicks complaining that they're "Not a girl . . . not yet a woman."

SPEED BUMP

If you've been using a celebrity's name for inspiration when you practice, you might find that it becomes ineffective after a while. It will seem as though it gets harder and harder to stay in touch with your inner Britney. This is actually a good thing, because it means that you're making progress. How so? You are more than the sum of your Britney parts: You are a combination of Britney's exhibitionism, Angelina's rebelliousness, and Ashley's intelligence. You are all of this and, most importantly, you. Therefore, you deserve a name all your own.

A Rose by Any Other Name . . .

"What's in a name?" Shakespeare asks, and the question makes sense—would the scent of a rose be so enigmatic if it had a different name? The real point, of course, is that it's the total package that makes a rose what it is: the vibrancy of its color, its scent, its name, the somewhat shocking nature of its thorns.

The same goes for celebrities and their pop personas. Think about Madonna. Madonna is a sacred name, the emblem of tender, maternal love bestowed on a brassy, pop-culture mercenary. Yet it's this contradiction between the sacred and the profane that makes Madonna the focus of endless fascination. Would Madonna be the subject of introductory college courses around the country if her name were Beth?

EXERCISE: WHAT'S MY NAME? (PART I)

You will need: some quiet time, a notebook or journal, and a pen.

Begin by sitting quietly. Do a few deep breaths to center yourself. Let any thoughts or concerns gently wash over you as you let them go. Then pick up your journal and pen and write down the answers to the following questions:

1. What is my body type? (E.g., athletic, waif, top-heavy, apple, or pear.)

2. Who are the young, hot celebrities that currently share my body type? (IMPORTANT NOTE: It doesn't matter if you are overweight or not. You can still share Jennifer Garner's body type even if you have fifty extra pounds on top of it.)

3. What body part or areas do you focus on when you dance? For example, you probably noticed that when you've done your practice dances—or even when you've danced for your

man—that you've tended to play up certain areas. Some might put the emphasis on their heinies, while others put the emphasis on their hooters. Still others like to show off a tight set of abs, or to highlight their shapely legs.

At this point, stop for a second and think about what you've written. Does your personal body type, or any of the celebrities you share it with, conjure up any images? For example, maybe you realize that with your pale skin and rounded body you resemble an artist's model in a Renaissance painting. You might then feel a connection to names that reflect this, like Francesca, Gabrielle, or Celeste. Write down whatever pops into your head. Then ask yourself the following:

4. What are my top five all-time favorite songs to dance to? If you practiced giving a dance or have actually danced for your man, write down the names of the songs that you danced to as well. The practicality of the song doesn't matter. For example, I have probably given the best lap dances of my life to absolutely no one, in the privacy of my living room, to the following songs: "Shamalamma Ding Dong" by Otis Day and the Knights, "Tipitina" by Professor Longhair, and "All You Ever Do Is Bring Me Down" by the Mavericks.

So even though I dance to mostly metal at the club, my favorite music tends to be fifties and sixties R&B. Go figure. Once you have the list, think about what kind of music you gravitate to. Once again, let whatever images and connections these songs evoke come naturally to mind. For me, when I dance to "Shamalamma

Ding Dong" I imagine myself alone with my man in a dark, smoky blues club. I also imagine (I'm not sure why) that I have long, curly dark hair and am wearing a strapless blue cocktail dress. In my fantasy, I have so much pent-up lust and longing for him that I can't control it any longer, and when that special song comes on, I have no other choice but to express myself by dancing for him.

5. How does the information you have so far connect with the different dancer looks? For example, the underlying theme of my "Shamalamma Ding Dong" fantasy is the need to express myself sexually, to dominate. This fits in well with the Video Vixen persona. Write down the one look that you feel best represents who you are. Now, you might have a hard time narrowing it down to just one look, and that's okay. Strippers aren't formed in cookie-cutter molds—we all have unique quirks and qualities that we bring to the dance. We're just looking for your dominant traits here. For instance, I might be a particularly sarcastic Video Vixen, but I'm still every inch a Video Vixen. Just like you might be a California Girl with a materialistic streak.

Once you have your stripper look, it's time to find your stripper name.

Again, settle yourself somewhere comfortable, and focus your breathing on your belly. (If you do yoga or meditation, focus your breathing on your lowest chakra.) As you breathe, call up your sexual energy. Breathe into it as though you were breathing life into a fire. Let it bubble and course through you. When you really start to feel it, ask yourself this question: What is my stripper name? It's possible that it'll come to you right away. It's also possible that several ideas will pop into your head at once. If this is the case, just write them all down in your journal. If you have the time, sift through each one, trying it on for size, until you arrive at the one that feels the most right. If you don't have the time right now, feel free to take an hour, a day, or a week to think about each one to come up with the perfect fit.

EXERCISE: WHAT'S MY NAME? (PART II)

You will need: some quiet time, a notebook or journal, and a pen.

Now that you have a name for your inner hottie, it's time to get to know her. Ask her: What do you like about your body? What do you like about sex? What are your fantasies and desires? Be open to whatever thoughts come up. Be warned, however: Some of your answers might shock you. If this is the case, try not to judge yourself—even if images of whipping your husband with a riding crop spring to mind. After all, unleashing your inner hottie is about release. Whatever unexplored fantasies or desires you have are all okay, because they're all part of you. At a later date, think about what you learned about yourself during this exercise. For example, if you realized that you really wanted to have sex in your car or on the kitchen table, then think about ways to make it happen. If you learned something unsettling, like that you're attracted to your boss, then think about ways you can fulfill the desire in fantasy, or by role-playing with your partner.

The most important part is that you accept whatever it is that comes up, because it's only through self-acceptance that we are able to really own and appreciate our sexuality. So work extra hard to be kind to yourself.

GETTING IT DONE

Inner hottie is just a term I've coined to describe the locus of your sexual energy—the special, specific kind of energy you possess as a woman. Strippers know how to harness and package this energy for a living, but the truth is that all of us tap into it from time to time, consciously or not. The rituals we go through—putting on makeup, picking out an outfit—are *how* we tap into this energy. This is how hotties get things done.

Let's review: When you truly own your sexuality (along with every other part of yourself) you are bringing your whole self to the table. You're able to rely on and utilize each and every part of yourself to get stuff done. Remember the scene in *Erin Brockovich* when Masry, Erin's boss, asks her how she will be able to get some key piece of evidence? She calmly looks at him and replies, "They're called boobs, Ed." Erin wasn't afraid to use her sexuality (i.e., her inner hottie) to get results. You shouldn't be either.

MORE SOURCES FOR INSPIRATION

A couple of years ago, a women's magazine pointed out in passing that Condoleezza Rice was hot. I was a little shocked, because it actually hadn't occurred to me to look past the whole national security adviser thing. The more I thought about it, though, the more I realized that the magazine was right. Any way you slice it, Condoleezza Rice is a hottie. Part of what makes her hot is the fact that she doesn't force it. Hotties embrace their hotness, but they don't desperately cling to it, either. Here is a short list of celebrities who are in touch with their hotness.

Hotties:

PAMELA ANDERSON: The pioneer of being hot for hotness's sake.

MARIAH CAREY: Could add a yard of fabric to every single one of her outfits and still look like a stripper on a smoke break. Still, she's honest and unapologetic about her look.

JAMIE LEE CURTIS: Fearlessly exposed her cellulite in a national women's magazine.

JANET JACKSON: Survived being a child star *and* being a member of the Jackson clan.

LUCY LIU: Shows in her acting roles that you can be strong, bitchy, and mercilessly hot all at the same time.

DEMI MOORE: At forty years old was unafraid to take boy toy Ashton Kutcher to satisfy her wanton needs.

MICHELLE PFEIFFER: Low-key, unforced beauty.

BRITNEY SPEARS: Brimming with natural sexual energy that she just can't hide.

For every celebrity who is in touch with their inner hottie, there are at least ten who are not. These are the women who do their hair and makeup not for a source of strength but to offer a sort of apology for some real or imagined shortcoming.

Notties:

MELANIE GRIFFITH: A bad example for aging women everywhere. Too much surgery, too skinny, and way too possessive of Antonio.

SARAH JESSICA PARKER: And any other woman who gives

birth and can bounce a quarter off her rippled abs less than
six months later.

RENEE ZELLWEGER: Renee, along with any other female
star who purposefully gained weight for a role and then,
instead of just losing it, forced it off with such violence that
there was nothing left but pinched skin and jutting bone. I
mean, did you see *Chicago*? What the hell happened to her?

So, Grasshopper, let's review. You have gotten to know your inner
stripper, and you have named her. You also know how to get her
up on the main stage, to use her energy whenever you need it.
Through the examples of others who have gone before you, you
have learned that your hotness is like a magic candle: Care for it
properly, and the flame will guide you. Hold it too closely, and the
flame will burn out.

EXERCISE: TOP SECRET

Run an errand in your sweats, with your hair in a ponytail and no
makeup on. Be aware of the people around you, how they react to
and notice you. After you have a sense of this, shift your awareness to the fact that you are plain old Jane Smith by day and
Tatiana, Mistress of Desire, by night. As you view the people near
you, how does it feel to know that you have a secret identity as a
sex goddess? Do you feel powerful? Sexy? Silly?

How would those around you react if they saw you as your
inner hottie right now?

EXERCISE: BLOW YOUR COVER

Spend at least an hour as Tatiana, Amber, or Tiffany. Go about
your day—for example, buying the paper and coffee, purchasing

your ticket and riding the train to work—as your inner stripper. All the while, be conscious of yourself and how you interact with others. Note the differences between how you act and feel when you are just being yourself and when you are being your inner hottie.

A word of caution, though: Act too hot, and total strangers might start asking you for a lap dance!

CONCLUSION

On the journey to unleashing your inner hottie, it's important to remember these few things:

1. DANCERS ARE MADE, NOT BORN

Feeling comfortable with your body takes a lot of practice. Don't get down on yourself by thinking that there are some women (strippers, models) who are naturally hot and don't have to work at it. That's just not true. Every woman has something she feels insecure about. If you are not comfortable with your own unique beauty, you are not hot. So do the exercises in the book as often as you can, and give yourself some patience and room to grow.

2. FEELING INSECURE IS A CHOICE

You don't have to love everything about your body—but you don't have to hate it either. Fix what you can and find a way to let go of the rest of it. Letting your insecurities go will free up emotional space for self-acceptance.

3. MAKE TAKING CARE OF YOURSELF A PRIORITY

When you look good, you feel good. Stop making excuses for why you haven't shaved your legs in three weeks. Sure, you save a few extra minutes a day, but is it worth turning down sex for? For that matter, is it worth not being able to enjoy the feeling of your own legs when they are nice and smooth? Find the time to care for yourself.

4. DRESS FOR SEXCESS

Dressing well is part of how we take care of ourselves. By making even minor changes to your wardrobe, you can make your man go from lame to untamed. Better yet, you'll also feel more confident and sexy. Switch a white tee for a fitted tee, or wear a denim skirt instead of shorts. By dressing like a hottie, you'll feel like a hottie.

5. FLIRT!

When you truly own your sexuality, you're not afraid to flaunt it. Remember, this is the real reason that men love strippers! So flirt with your man, tease him, taunt him, make him beg. Revel in all the glorious power you have as a woman, and let him know who's really in charge.

6. KNOW THYSELF

Finally, getting to know yourself (and your inner hottie) is a life-long process filled with rewards. She may shock, surprise, or even alarm you, but at least you'll know that you (and your man) will never, ever be bored.

ABOUT THE AUTHOR

Jessica "Kayla" Conrad was a dancer at New York's world-famous gentlemen's club Scores. She is a wife, mother, student, and author, and lives in Bronxville, New York.

HQ